COVIDOLOGY

COVIDOLOGY

SHARING LIFE LESSONS
FROM BEHIND THE MASK

EDITED BY PAUL IARROBINO

COVIDOLOGY is set in Calluna and Calluna Sans.

Distributed in partnership with:
Windtree Press
https://windtreepress.com

ISBN EBOOK 978-1-957638-28-7
ISBN PAPERBACK 978-1-957638-29-4

This anthology is dedicated to everyone who attended our virtual pandemic groups, where "gratitude, resilience, and connection" became our cheerleading mantra to avoid the "pity party."

Obstacles don't block the path.
They are *the path.*

—Zen proverb

Table of Contents

ACKNOWLEDGMENTS

Thanks to my husband, Arnel Mandilag, for putting up with my never-ending avalanche of projects and sticking by me through all of them, especially this one. I value his grounding presence, attention to detail, and expert technological and design skills. His talents make the pages and cover of this book shine. Thanks, baby!

Jim Sutherland and I have been friends for over thirty years. Who would have thought when we met in 1991, he would go on to author two books (*Love, Your Mother – Like It or Not* and *Tangled Webs*). Jim served as a writing coach and editor for this anthology. I am grateful for his mentorship and friendship. I look forward to reading his next book.

I didn't know Sittrea Friberg well before this project but I have now gained a new friend and "aunt" in the process. Sittrea is the kindest writing coach and editor out there. Her years of facilitating book groups and offering editing advice to authors have uniquely prepared her for this project. She's enlightening me and other anthology contributors of the other meaning of "speed bumps." I am pleased to learn new writing and coaching skills from Sittrea.

I am fortunate to have been mentored by author and co-founder of Windtree Press, Maggie Lynch. Maggie walked me through the complicated, ever-changing world of publishing like a seasoned industry tour guide. She's incredibly resourceful and I am honored to join her and fellow authors at Windtree. It's like being adopted by a large extended family of literary masters.

I am grateful to the following friends who also served as beta readers: Laurie Olson, Tami Cockeram, and Scott Strickland. Their invaluable feedback provided necessary insight in the final days of review just prior to publishing.

And finally, a big thank you to our authors and poets for submitting their work and trusting in the process. Without you we wouldn't have an anthology. Thank you!

PREFACE

Unlike the unpredictable course of the pandemic, this anthology is the result of strangers willing to create a new path of embracing our vulnerabilities, digging deep, and engaging in meaningful and often humorous conversations. It's this camaraderie that planted the seeds for this artistic and literary endeavor.

COVID came with it many surprises for me to personally examine. Having clarity in my life in a way I never experienced before is a clear takeaway. I am extremely grateful for that.

What credentials do I have to be a first-time author? None! I added to and expanded my toolbox over these past few years and surrounded myself with incredibly supportive souls, also working through similar shifts during these bumpy times. These interactions made this all possible.

It's my hope this book reaches you deeply, inspires a sense of curiosity and contributes to a sense of calm and well-being.

—Paul Iarrobino

INTRODUCTION

Some of the darkest moments of my life happened in March 2020. Getting COVID in the early days of pandemic infection brought a unique set of challenges I hadn't encountered before. Do I dare tell anyone and bear the risk of being branded with a modern-day scarlet letter? Besides, without an antigen test, the best advice given at the time was to isolate. That's exactly what I did. The ever-changing symptoms of fever, chills, extreme fatigue, body aches, headaches, and congestion wiped me out. Depression also set in when all of my work as a self-employed performer, event producer, and community volunteer vanished during those few weeks. What's the use of feeling better when all my life's work has been taken away?

I took a chance on Zoom. Virtual connections quickly became my new world. I found that while there was a real need for us to connect in meaningful ways during the early days of lockdown, we lacked the experience and confidence of connecting in virtual spaces.

I started facilitating these small group meetings, mostly with older adults. The personality of each group was uniquely different but served as an important lifeline to a new world that didn't come with a user manual.

These rich conversations served as a creative spark to write my own story while encouraging others to do the same. It's my hope these stories will help you realize and appreciate the important shifts you have made, remember what really matters in your life, and how you want to live your best life moving forward.

Each story or poem is told by everyday people like you and me, and no two are alike. We were faced with situations during a deadly pandemic and had to make decisions with a different set of criteria. How would you respond in situations like this?

Your beloved spouse passes away and you are not permitted to have an in-person memorial. Do you have it on Zoom or wait and hope an-person gathering will be allowed some time in the future?

What if your spouse has dementia and you are exhausted from providing 24/7 care, but are afraid you won't see them if the facility goes into lockdown?

What if your parent dies, lives 3000 miles away and you not only have to take flights to get there, but your family and loved ones won't be masked up at the service at the small, rural home, when you religiously wear your mask in crowds?

What about the extra time COVID gave us? Were you able to do something you always dreamed of but never had the time? What if that extra time created a potential new path? Would you take it?

I encourage you to personally reflect on these contributions and see what resonates for you.

A Million Miles from Here

by Stacey Rice

There are things you take for granted when living in the Pacific Northwest. You can bet that when November rolls around, the daily misting rain will start and not end until April, if you are lucky. When you round a corner in Portland, Oregon you will get a glimpse of Mt. Hood staring back at you in all its snow covered, iconic mountain glory. That's when I gasp and utter "Holy crap!" for the umpteenth time. I just can't believe that big mountain is right there.

It was a little over eleven years ago when I first laid eyes on Portland and the Pacific Northwest. I stood on the busy curb at the airport waiting for my friends to pick me up. I watched the airport traffic swirl in front of me, and I stood aside as people rushed by.

I found myself being lifted up into a faraway quiet space. The soft air surrounding me had a familiarity which passed straight through my heart. It was a feeling of something long forgotten. I wondered if perhaps in a previous life, I had breathed that same soft air now filling up my lungs.

I slid into the back seat of my friend's car. We made our way through the busy city streets, dodging a light rail train or two. We drove past deep green conifer trees growing bigger than any I had seen before. As I gazed up at the overcast sky slowly gliding by my window, all I could think was "I have been here before." That feeling washing over me was deeper than my soul could wrap itself around. I felt I had finally come back home.

During the week I spent visiting with my dear friends, I realized I didn't want to go back to the life I had built for my transgender-self in North Carolina. When I thought about my life there, I felt tired. I was tired of fighting the daily struggle to keep myself out of harm's way. Living in a region of the country which can be unaccepting of people who are different, is exhausting.

I was tired of being closeted in my work life. I was not out to the people who lived in my condominium complex, or to any of my acquaintances. I was never sure just how accepting they would be of me. I could see living my life here in Portland would be much easier.

Almost every person I met during that week asked me, "You are moving here, aren't you?"

During the first days of my stay, I would tentatively say, "Well, maybe." But by the end, I knew I wanted to move here.

Six months later I did.

It was a couple of months before my moving date, and I started thinking about the long drive to Portland. How was I going to do it by myself? I thought of my friend Frankie and wondered if she would consider making the journey with me.

I called and asked if she would come with me for support by helping with driving and just being a good travel buddy. I was delighted when she said yes.

A few days later, she called me back and shouted,

"Stacey, Portland is on the other side of the country!"

My dear Frankie hadn't looked at the map before she agreed to come with me. She was in a state of disbelief at how far away Oregon was. After some persuasion on my part, and after her initial shock wore off, she agreed, "Okay, I will come with you."

On an early frost filled morning in late February, I picked up Frankie and we eased ourselves onto I-40 West. I was heading out of the Blue Ridge Mountains which had held me close for most of my life. But I knew deep in my heart, I was heading towards a life which was going to be better.

The drive across the country with Frankie was full of the most wonderful adventures. Every so often, we would look at each other and laugh. This trip was just like the movie "Thelma and Louise." We had the sunglasses, but we veered off script: we didn't commit any murders or robberies along the way.

In Tennessee, we found ourselves at Sun Studios in Memphis. We walked through the front door and into a room which held more hillbilly dust than you could imagine. We stood in the very spot on that worn, linoleum tile floor where Elvis had sung all his early songs.

We sped 85 miles per hour across the pancake flat panhandle of Texas. There we stopped at a combination gas station/Subway restaurant in the middle of nowhere. Then we saw two cowboys ride up on their horses in the pasture next to the Subway. They tied their horses to the fence and went in to order a sandwich. "Howdy ma'am," they both said to Frankie and I as they walked by.

In New Mexico, we left the interstate and drove onto Route 66. The old road took us past house after house with red chili ristras hanging like tasty stalactites, just waiting to be dropped into a red chili sauce.

Then Frankie spotted a small apartment building and swung around in her seat. Looking intently into my eyes, she said, "If I ever disappear from my life and you wonder where I am, this is the first place you should look."

After six and a half long days of driving we arrived. At the intersection of Interstate 84 and Interstate 5, the city of Portland was laid out before us. I stole a glance at the trip odometer, and it showed we had driven 3,004 miles from my North Carolina front door. Little did I know on that day, in the early spring of 2012, those 3,004 miles would feel like a million miles in 2020.

It was a few months into the pandemic, when I realized there was something very precious I had taken for granted. Something more than the never-ending rain and the majestic Mt. Hood that had become part of my life here. It was the unacknowledged realization that I would always be able to see my family back in North Carolina whenever I wanted.

My daughter and her family live in central North Carolina, between the mountains to the west and the coastal plain to the east. It gets hot as blue blazes in the summertime. There is a smothering humidity that drapes your body like a wet blanket.

Those mountains to the west, held my 89-year-old dad, my brother and his family. All nestled in those tall, rounded, ancient blue mountains that fill up that part of the world. Just like clockwork, every year, I would fly back a couple of times to visit them for a week or so

Then COVID made itself known. In June 2020, I lost my job and found myself quarantined and socially isolated. There was no workplace to connect to, no partner to be with, and no friends to visit. They were as tightly quarantined as I was. As I sat on my sofa early one morning in mid-June, it hit me. I was thinking about my family and how far away they were at that moment. I realized there was no way I could go see them because of the epidemic. I started to cry.

Deep, deep sobs. "I am so alone," was all I could say to myself over and over through my tears. A deep, soul-crushing loneliness and isolation overwhelmed me. I wasn't sure I could get over it.

Loneliness and I have been friends for a pretty long time. We first got to know each other when I was around five years old. It was then I understood the world around me saw a little boy and not the little girl I knew I was inside. My days for a very long time were filled with a crippling anxiety and an aloneness that often overwhelmed me. All I could think was, "I must be the only one in the whole world that feels this way."

The loneliness and anxiety I experienced during those decades before my transition, twenty years before, came back with a vengeance on that day in mid-June. How could I be at this place once again?

My mind started racing. What if I get sick with COVID? What if I die alone? Whenever I felt a slight scratch in my throat, or I had to cough, I panicked. I was sure this was the beginning of COVID. Do I have a fever? Good Lord, I don't even have a thermometer. What about my family? Are they safe?

Despite all of my fears, I started to hatch a plan to go back to my family, even if just for a little while. There was no way I was going to get on a plane with my risk factors. I had had a heart attack and heart bypass surgery five years before. After all that damage, I didn't have a whole heart left to be attacked any more.

However, I did fantasize about going through TSA with my carry on. Once on the other side, I saw myself opening it up and pulling out a hazmat suit and respirator which I would put on. That would protect me. However, I wasn't sure what the airline would think about a passenger traveling in a hazmat suit. I pictured my fellow travelers, befuddled and all jealous they hadn't thought of my brilliant idea first. Would I even be able to go through TSA Pre-Check if I did this?

Everyday my life began to resemble a movie. This time, "Planes, Trains, and Automobiles." I studied train schedules and researched quarantining options of a sleeper accommodation.

The more I searched for answers, the more questions I had. What does an RV cost to rent? Could I camp out of the back of one? What about a rental car? How many days would it take me to get back closer to my loved ones?

I continued to pour over my maps. It took a while before I realized that none of this was going to work. The strength of the pandemic restrictions, the amount of money and length of time needed to make this trip was just going to be too much.

However, something larger than the pandemic and my fear of pandemic flying, finally took me back home to my family. It was a phone call. My dad called me the previous fall and told me he was tired. He was tired of living and struggling with a myriad of long-term health issues. He was tired of the social isolation he had been living with since the pandemic started. He said, "I just want to go see your mom. It's been so long." My mother passed away many, many years ago. I understood in my heart what he was saying. He was truly ready to go.

A couple of months later, he passed on. I found myself heading back home to those North Carolina mountains that I love; pandemic flying be damned. I was on my way to say goodbye to the man whom I loved so much. It was my dad who had, against so many odds, accepted his transgender daughter.

I thought about the day, so long ago, when I first shared with my dad I was transgender and I was going to eventually transition to my female self.

The first words out of his mouth were, "I wish you wouldn't do this."

Then he asked, "Isn't there a pill you can take for this?"

I remember being a bit amused by his question about a pill. I answered him, "Yes there is Dad. It is called estrogen."

He struggled with what I was doing and becoming. It took some time for us to work through it all.

He was a man born in the early 1930's and who lived his whole life in those mountains steeped in a conservative culture. But he hung in there because of the love he had for his daughter. Despite the fears he had, his thoughts about what people would say, and all the things he didn't understand, in the end, it was his unconditional love for me which overcame it all. This was the most beautiful gift he could have given me.

Little did I know when I arrived back home for his funeral, that his gift of acceptance would continue after his death.

From my socially isolated pandemic home in Portland, I was suddenly thrust into spaces filled with people. So many people. People who had known me long before my transition, over twenty years ago. Most had not laid eyes on me since then. They included my many cousins and other relatives. There were also longtime friends of the family, like the woman who cut my hair when I was a teenager, and people I went to high school with. And the plumber who plumbed the houses I built back in my previous male life, along with so many others.

My mind was reeling with expectations, but I was also cautiously on guard. I could not help but wonder, "What are people's reactions going to be? What will I have to deal with? When and where will I have to stand up for myself?"

But like the beautiful gift of love and acceptance that my dad had given to me, I was soon surrounded by that same love and acceptance from everyone I met over those next few days.

Their words of how happy they were to see me after all these years were a balm to my soul. And I could just picture my dad smiling because he had set the best example of all.

Stacey is a speaker, educator and consultant and a community leader on transgender issues. She was recognized in 2016 as a Queer Hero NW by the Gay and Lesbian Archives of the Pacific NW and is the former Executive Co-Director of Q Center, the largest LGBTQ+ community center in the Pacific Northwest. More info on Stacey can be found at www.staceyrice.com.

What? I'm Not in Charge?

by Carol Brownlow

Greetings fellow pandemic survivors. We have witnessed something we hope to never see again, illness, death, confusion, and misunderstanding.

I am eighty years old. If you asked me two years ago to tell you *who I was*, I would have definitely said, I was a self-directed, independent woman in charge of my life. I knew who I was. I had been that person for a long time. Then along came COVID. So many things happened which revealed, much to my surprise, I am not in charge of my life. I am, in fact, sometimes the victim of circumstances beyond my control. I have often said there are three kinds of people in this world: *those who make it happen, those who watch it happen and those who wonder what happened.* I always prided myself in being one who *made it happen.* I had been the coach, the professor, and the dean. I was accustomed to getting what I wanted.

Once we were in the throes of the pandemic, however, I had to face the reality that I could not always *make things happen.* I became frustrated and humbled. I did not know how to cope.

I am one of the lucky ones; I never contracted COVID. Some of my friends became ill and very debilitated. Yet, the epidemic had a profound impact on my life.

I was the primary care provider for a friend. I moved her into a new assisted living facility just as COVID was invading Oregon. She had dementia and I wanted to see that she received the best care possible. The facility rules were very controlling and restrictive.

The only way I could visit her was if staff brought her from her cottage to a central building, and then we had to talk through an open window. Because of her dementia, she could not comprehend what was happening. All she knew was I had dumped her in a strange place. I had abandoned her.

She didn't own a cell phone (nor could she operate one) so in-person conversations were our only recourse. The situation was a real inconvenience and very stressful for both of us.

The care facility staff was scared. They were understaffed and were doing all they could to prevent COVID from ravaging their residents. However, to those of us on the outside, we experienced their actions only as unreasonable and cruel.

It was humbling to learn I had absolutely NO say in whatever they decided to do. Including, how they did it, when I could or could not visit and for how long. How frustrating for someone who had for years been the boss and called the shots.

I vacillated between frustration and anger. I finally reconciled with reality. I had become one of those individuals who was *watching what happened or wondering what happened.* Eventually, I had to accept that *they* were in charge; that I had no power at all. This was unfamiliar territory for me.

I really felt the impact of the epidemic when it offered me the opportunity to examine my priorities. I was transitioning from a human *doing* to a human *being.* You may argue that was not bad. However, for me, it was an unwelcome change. Who was I if I could not be out and about, getting things done, making things happen?

The first few months of isolation I filled my time with projects. I researched my genealogy and wrote to the majority of my many cousins. I organized my earthquake preparedness kit. I made a "to do" list as I had always done. I checked items off the list and relished my accomplishments. I was still doing things. I was living my usual busy schedule, but with one big void. I had no in-person interaction with others. This was a new challenge for me.

As the months dragged on, as the rules changed, as the opportunities to socialize dwindled, I grew less and less obsessed with *getting things done*. I became more and more uncomfortable with my life.

My sisters worried about my lack of connection with my friends, so they invited me to "bubble dinners." They started calling me more frequently so I would not feel so alone.

I was accustomed to eating out frequently. When the epidemic closed most of the restaurants, I secretly thought I might develop an interest in, or perhaps even an appreciation for cooking. That, however, did not happen. I resorted to eating TV dinners and easy to prepare meals. I snacked too much and gained weight. It was evident I did not know how to be by myself. Fortunately, I did not get depressed nor resort to drinking or taking drugs. In my heart, I kept hoping things would "return to normal." I knew how to do normal, very well.

After over six hundred rounds of Genies and Gems, six hundred forty-three rounds of Jewels Magic Lamp, and progressing to level five hundred-fourteen of Solitaire—all played on the computer—I had become an iPad junkie.

Next, I re-discovered streaming on Netflix, and began watching countless new movies and TV shows. I even bought a new recliner to replace my old and uncomfortable loveseat. Now I could settle in for hours.

Prior to COVID, my life had included lots of dancing, movies, plays and eating in nice restaurants, potlucks, and Happy Hours. But as a result of social isolation, I had turned into a stay-at-home introvert. I learned to slow down, to ignore "to do lists" and be okay with watching TV—sometimes even during the day. Some days, I even managed to have breakfast, exercise, and get dressed by noon. Urgency had become a stranger.

If all of these challenges were not enough, I was also scheduled to have major surgery in the early fall of 2021. The night before I was to be admitted, the hospital called to postpone. My surgery was delayed for two months because of the bed shortage in the hospital. COVID had overwhelmed the medical services.

Up until two days before the actual surgery, I did not know whether or not it would happen. As a result of the delay, all my pre-surgery tests had to be redone, all the arrangements for help at home had to be rescheduled and all transportation requests of friends had to be rearranged. Once again, COVID was *making things happen*, not me.

***

When Socrates said, "Know thyself," he surely must have meant before, during and after a pandemic. Riding the roller-coaster of mask on, mask off, social distancing (how close is too close), restaurants open, restaurants closed, get a booster, no need to get a booster became an exercise in acceptance, flexibility, and resilience. I thought I knew myself, but I had become a stranger in my own life.

Let me repeat. I am one of the lucky ones. I live in a senior community where every precaution was taken to avoid the infection, and we were successful.

As weeks turned into months and eventually into years, I had become more content to stay home, to play computer games, and to read. Lately, I have begun to venture out into the community again. I remember before the pandemic, restaurants were noisy. I find now that noise in social gatherings is something I really don't tolerate well. I just don't enjoy all the hubbub. Traffic is more intimidating. My fear of anti-vaxxers is real.

Are these reactions a result of my having more quiet time? Do I blame them on the pandemic? Or as time passes, am I just turning into a cranky old woman?

I admit to having COVID FATIGUE. I'm tired of the rules continually changing. I want the isolation to be over. The sadness of losing friends is wearing me down.

I'm getting old. I don't want my precious remaining years to be spent here alone in this apartment. Who will I be when the outside world feels safe again? Will I be able to go back to being the old me? Or will I be the new me—the woman who *makes things happen* again? What say you, Socrates?

Carol Brownlow is a retired educator and strong advocate for LGBTQ+ Seniors in Oregon. She serves on the SAGE Metro Portland Housing Committee.

She also facilitates a support group for lesbians over age 70 and provides leadership for the Gay & Grey community in her retirement housing.

Her hobbies include golf, dancing, and live theater. She writes poetry and participates in readers theater. She has participated in storytelling, but finds her comfort level higher sharing the written word.

Carol lives at Rose Villa Retirement Community in Portland, Oregon.

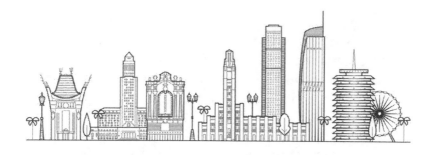

Navigating My Emotional Labyrinth Without A GPS

by Russell Alexander-Orozco

As Friday noon approached, I rushed out of my temporary job in Pasadena, not even leaving myself time to grab lunch. I was anxious since this was my first time maneuvering a seventeen-mile jaunt across town in Los Angeles traffic. I had two crucial appointments ahead of me—one with my doctor and the other with Being Alive, a non-profit where I volunteer.

The warmth of the mid-day sun, just prior to unfolding into spring, was a welcome delight after being cooped up in a busy office all morning. I decided to drive in silence, no radio, no singing, no music, and definitely no news—just me, and the natural wonders of the road.

I wanted to be in a relaxed state because of the possibility of troubling news regarding my recent medical exams. I had allowed myself plenty of time, or so I thought.

Before long I could see in the distance, the sparkling and ever-changing skyline of downtown L.A. The U.S. Bank Tower is my favorite and the most iconic of all, with its all-glass crown top and observation deck. One thing about driving and chilling is that you have to make sure not to space out.

As I reached into my backpack for some smoked almonds to snack on, I looked over and noticed that there were an unusual number of cars backed up trying to merge onto the Interstate—quite a rare visual for the middle of the day. Then up ahead, I spotted the large signage for the highway exit that circumvents downtown. But for some unknown reason, I ended up taking the wrong exit and was unintentionally heading right into downtown.

It had been a while since I was spontaneous. I convinced myself this unplanned route would be an adventure I would enjoy. Time seemed to move quite quickly and so did the odometer. As I traveled into what was clearly unchartered territory, nothing looked memorable or inviting. I had no clue as to where this road would lead. It was now obvious I had entered a dodgy part of town, and I needed to recalibrate my directional bearings in order to reach my first appointment.

If a techie friend had joined me, they probably would have taken out their phones and used their GPS, something I had never tinkered with. In fact, up until six months earlier I was a proud owner of a blackberry phone, a relic of cellphones. Besides, if I needed assistance, I had my old reliable *Thomas Guide*, the spiral bound bible of road maps, predating electronic gadgets.

Frustration kicked in because I couldn't spot a landmark to use as my guide. That's when my self-talk kicked in.

Let's see Russell. All you need to do is head northwest. It's still early afternoon, so the sun is mostly south, which means the opposite is north. Now you can pinpoint where west is. Bingo, you're all set.

Problem was, the buildings were blocking the sun. Soon everything around me started to look the same. I suddenly felt claustrophobic. I couldn't decipher one block from another, and then I realized that I've been circling the same area for who knows how long.

I could feel the sweat dripping from my forehead. *Why is this happening to me? I'm the navigator. Everyone is always asking me for directions. I even offer them to my Uber driver.*

I was completely disoriented, caught in an urban labyrinth, without a clue as to which way was north, south, east, or west. The clock was ticking and if I was to make it to my first appointment, I needed to hurry. Doctor's offices aren't very forgiving, and it usually takes weeks to reschedule—it was crucial that I be punctual.

I pulled over to the side. I brought out my treasured *Thomas Guide*. And as I'm thumbing through it, I can't believe what I'm seeing—the page I want is missing. My body temperature goes clammy. My hands start shaking as I realize that I'm not only trapped, but I am on the verge of a major anxiety episode.

I did my best to center myself by taking a drink of water and repeating, "No harm will come to me, no harm will come to me." I had to call the doctor's office.

"I'm lost, I took a different route and I'm lost."

"Can you still come in?" Oddly enough, the receptionist seemed unfazed.

"Yes, but there's no way I can get there on time."

After a short pause, she informed me that the person scheduled after me had canceled and I could take their place. That should give me plenty of time.

I uttered a "Hallelujah!"

I needed to calm down. I took several deep breaths and called upon my guardian angel for guidance. I've relied on him since I was a kid. I waited for a sign. Nothing. I took more deep breaths, making sure they were really slow this time. Still nothing. I was struggling to stay focused. The clock was ticking. I closed my eyes and this time called upon both my guardian angel and my spirit guide. I wasn't about to take any chances.

Without missing a beat, I could feel the energy shift and I was back on the road. It's not like I hear voices, but there's no denying their presence and guidance. Before long, the sun was shining behind me as I headed northwest. What a relief when I pulled into the doctor's office parking lot, twenty minutes ahead of schedule.

I gathered myself so my heart was no longer pumping a mile a minute. Then it dawned on me I hadn't notified the office staff at Being Alive that I would be late for our appointment.

Being Alive is a tiny, non-profit social service agency doing essential work with the LGBTQ HIV community for the past thirty-three years. I've always respected their commitment. I recall the fun times I had hosting the ever popular "Hug a Hunk Booth" in the mid-90's at our LA Pride Fairs. Those were also heartbreaking times as so many around me continued to succumb to AIDS.

Today's appointment was crucial because as a volunteer consultant to Being Alive, I was going there to complete a strategic plan that would not only assure sustainability, but also promote the organization's growth. I'd been working with Garry, their CEO, for months and today we were finalizing some major time-lines. And what a gift. Through our work, we developed a great friendship. I also had a close camaraderie with his entire staff, leading to no shortage of hugs to go around, something I was looking forward to after a trying day like I was having.

I called and someone quickly answered. "Hi, it's Russell. I'm scheduled to meet Garry at 4 PM, but I won't be able to get there till around five. Can you let him know, please?"

After a slight pause, "No one is staying late tonight—we're following Mayor Garcetti's mandate."

I was utterly dumbfounded. It was Friday, March 13, 2020, and COVID-19 had arrived in full force. I had been completely oblivious to what was happening around me as I traveled across town. No wonder traffic was backed up getting onto the Interstate.

Within a few days, a "safer at home" health order was issued. None of us had any idea as to what was ahead.

The following week I received an alarming text from a close friend, informing me that Garry and his entire staff were experiencing COVID symptoms and they had to close the office. Within a few days all were extremely ill. Every night that followed, I went into prayer and lit candles, confident that they would make it through this.

Not long after, I received word that COVID had taken our dear Garry. I was heartbroken and completely aware that at any moment I could possibly begin to spiral emotionally.

Truth be told, I haven't been able to say the "d" word since my partner Paul passed away in 1992. I use *lost, taken, gone, passed or left—anything but dead*. I've had a long and difficult history dealing with grief, a type of PTSD that can manifest itself with deep somatic paralyzing symptoms. I lose all energy and desire to be creative, and joy becomes elusive. I've struggled with it for over thirty years, ever since the AIDS epidemic took so many friends and colleagues.

Thankfully the rest of Garry's staff recovered. That uplifting piece of welcomed news quickly became overshadowed when I learned that yet another close friend and admired colleague had died. I once again prepared for a major emotional tsunami of grief to overtake me. But time moved on and inexplicably those trigger symptoms kept their distance since Garry's passing. This was my first clue that a shift had occurred.

The pandemic was definitely the initial factor that forced me to slow down, but eclipsing it came about when I was diagnosed with cancer in the midst of all this chaos. The depth of my inner work, both emotionally and spiritually couldn't have been more synchronized. My inner child kicked me in the ass and said, *Let's take charge here.*

All the proactive work and energy that I've devoted to others was now going to be focused towards me. And so began a new journey of prioritizing Russell—I revived my meditation practice, participated in workshops and seminars, read books, took long walks, reconnected with old friends, and made new ones. I also wrote more, started yoga after a thirty-year absence and made sure that I was under the best medical care possible.

My perseverance was paying off as I could feel that I had ignited an inner transformation. I celebrated the news that the radiation treatments worked. The journey has not been all smooth sailing, particularly for someone like me who has mostly internalized his sentiments and presented a happy face.

The pivotal moment came when I embraced the fact that sharing my story was slowly becoming my healing partner. I was finally getting out of my own way and allowing myself the time to explore the depth of my emotions. I learned that sadness and grief need not be rushed or judged. I can now accept it's possible for me to have those feelings, without being paralyzed by them. And that I can indeed bask in joy when I remember all those wonderful souls that have been part of my life. In doing so, another milestone was taking place—the realization that I'm aging and accepting my own mortality.

I can now look back on this pandemic period with fortitude and eternal gratitude at having escaped COVID on Friday, March 13, 2020. Who would have ever imagined that being technically challenged and navigating my emotional labyrinth, without a GPS, would someday save my life?

Russell is a writer, actor, social advocate, and filmmaker.

He's an ongoing storyteller at L.A.'s Strong Words/Voices of the City. His screenplay A Star Is Dead *was a 2nd rounder at the Austin Film Festival Screenwriting Competition.*

His documentary, Mujeres Como Tu/Women Like You, *continues to make an impact in the HIV/AIDS field. Russell is an Executive Producer for the award-winning short film,* Sticky Pinecones.

He is also a certified Conscious Aging Facilitator and is developing the podcast, The Power of Aging—*celebrating exhilarating stories from our senior community.*

Russell no longer owns a Blackberry.

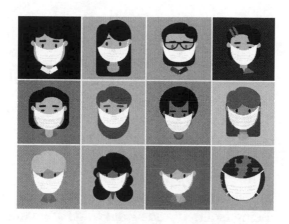

Pandemic Poems

by Carol Loo

April 2020

Too much time to think
Makes me want to sink
When will this end?
What's around the bend?
Where's the sun?
I'm not having fun
Wearing masks is now the norm
All the world is in this storm
This too shall pass is what I say
Praying for a rainbow day

May 2022

The pandemic is now a way of life
For so many people it's caused such strife
It's been a source of conflicting views
To get the vaccine and what to choose
To be 6 feet apart and to wear a mask
This is not an easy task
While looking back on the last 2 years
We've all had to face so many fears
Being isolated and afraid to go anywhere
What's happened to all of us doesn't seem fair
One had to look hard to find some pleasure
There's been an awareness of what we treasure
Being with others and feeling free
That's how I want it to always be

Prior to moving to Portland three years ago, Carol Loo spent more than fifty years in Kailua, on the island of Oahu. Her love for music and animals motivated her to volunteer giving piano lessons to people and attending to pets at the Hawaiian Humane Society. Carol was recognized with the Governor's Award as an "Outstanding Volunteer" saving countless numbers of otherwise healthy pets.

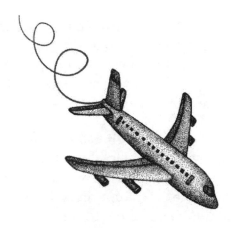

Tailspin

by Jamison Green

I used to be a traveler, a frequent flier, a globetrotter, closely monitoring my airline and hotel points. I was constantly aware of flight schedules and routes from the various airports I frequented on several continents. I attended meetings and conferences. I flew into cities to speak at corporate offices, medical clinics, government offices, conference centers, and research facilities. Sometimes, I even visited with friends between appointments.

Most often, I was in and out quickly. I loved to see people. I enjoyed speaking and contributing my ideas to projects. I took pleasure in sharing a fine meal or coffee or a glass of wine with colleagues from all over the world. I really loved the motion of travel, the logistics, the energy, the acts of arriving and departing, and the sensation of just getting somewhere.

Just in the last four months of 2019, my law and policy advocacy and educational efforts on behalf of transgender people took me to eight US cities and two foreign countries. My work also required three trips to Washington D.C. In January 2020, I visited Austin, Texas, and in February, I flew twice to the San Francisco Bay Area.

On Sunday, March 1st, after returning to Portland, the closest airport to my home in Vancouver Washington, I was relieved there were no trips planned for the next few months. I had writing to do at home on policy papers, and I was developing a book about the history of transgender medicine.

For the next few weeks, though, it was difficult to focus on my writing. I kept hearing on the radio about increasing concern over an infectious respiratory disease which had mysteriously appeared in Washington state. The news kept reporting that people were dying and doctors didn't know how to treat this COVID thing. There was no cure, only confusion, disbelief, concern, and fear. The medical providers and scientists among my colleagues were on alert. All were watchful, wary, and wanted to respond in helpful ways.

The teachers I knew were waiting for instructions: would schools close? How would the children be kept safe? The national corporations and law firms I worked with, along with the local retail stores and restaurants, seemed to be holding their collective breath. Then, the grocery stores started experiencing waves of panic buying. If you weren't fast enough, you might not find toilet paper, flour, or canned soup.

By March 23, 2020, instead of traveling in and out of airport terminals around the world, I was tethered to a different kind of terminal. The one at my desk. A *Stay-At-Home* order issued that day by Governor Inslee, was supposed to last for two weeks. The world outside my home stood still. The streets were quiet. It became a mini-vacation, a staycation.

I have asthma, and a healthy fear of suffocation. A deadly respiratory virus was a real threat to me. Air travel did not seem like a healthy option. A trip to Atlanta in May was canceled, along with every other trip already planned for that year.

I thought staying at home for a while would be just fine. Suddenly, I was negotiating schedules for the same number of engagements, but employing a different kind of travel, ironically called Zoom.

Zoom, and other video calling technologies, such as Skype and Web-Ex, were not new to me. My colleagues and I, scattered around the globe, used all of these programs frequently. I wasn't intimidated. I was going to be fine.

I spent those first two quiet weeks responding to email requests for Zoom meetings and juggling my schedule to accommodate all the conferences that were being reconfigured on video platforms.

My wife, Heidi, had already been working at home for many years as an instructional designer for a variety of training programs. At first it was just business as usual. But soon her clients were desperately seeking solutions to training problems they had never before encountered, because almost everyone was working remotely. Hours and hours of existing live classroom training modules had to be quickly redesigned, updated, and converted to online formats. In our working experience, this would be the first time a business slow-down did not result in the elimination of all training budgets. Instead, training via virtual meetings and conferences became the answer to every business problem. In no time, both Heidi and I were busier than ever!

Two weeks after the *Stay-At-Home* order was issued, Heidi and I needed a break from our home-offices. We decided to take a road trip out to South Bend, on the southwest Washington coast, a small town where my father had been born. I had never been there. My father never said much about the place because his parents moved to Los Angeles before he started school. Then, the family moved to Portland when he was twelve.

Heidi and I are both native Californians. I was familiar with much of Oregon because of family visits, and I attended university there. But neither of us had explored Washington beyond the Interstate 5 corridor when we'd visit Heidi's sister in Seattle. We'd moved to Vancouver from the San Francisco Bay area just two years earlier, and between working and getting settled, we hadn't gotten out much. Heidi and I thought a little road trip would be a nice way to spend the day. We'd get some fresh air, have a change of scenery, and I could satisfy a low-level curiosity about my dad's earthly launching point. We packed a couple of water bottles, some cheese and crackers and carrot sticks, and I put a fresh cup of coffee in my travel mug. With a full tank of gas, we were off.

There was hardly anyone on the city streets, or on the freeway. A few cars passed us going in the opposite direction on the state highway which led to the coast. The day was overcast and gray. We drove by open fields, forests, and farms. We saw nothing commercial or industrial until we reached Longview. Heading west, and then north, we followed the Columbia River toward the sea.

Among the commercial enterprises, gas stations, roadside stands, and coffee shops we passed, very few appeared open for business. We were traveling in what seemed to be abandoned or untouched territory. Humanity was strangely absent, and we felt unsettled and disconnected from the landscape. Watching through our car windows was like watching a still photo projected onto a screen. The only movement was our own.

I was reminded of the long-distance backpacking I'd done in the High Sierra, where one could go for days without seeing another soul. But this experience was qualitatively different. We were in civilization, in a moving vehicle. Where were all the people one would expect to see?

"I guess they really meant 'Stay-At-Home,' huh?" Heidi asked.

"Yeah," I replied. "It's eerie, I mean, I know we're going out through some sparsely populated country, but this is the Twilight Zone out here."

Heidi nodded. "It's kinda pretty, though," she said, hopefully.

"Yeah, if you like desolation."

"Come on, it's not that bad!" Heidi always looks for the good in any person or situation. I tend to wait for evidence.

"I like the rolling hills and the forests, and knowing that the river is just off there, not far away," I said, tipping my head toward the left where I knew the river flowed. "But I worry we really shouldn't be driving around out here. I mean, we're staying in our car and we're not breathing on anyone, but do you think we could get a ticket or be arrested or something?"

"I never heard anything like that. All they said was, 'Stay-At-Home' unless you have to go out for some essential reason," Heidi declared. "They never said you can't go out at all. As far as I'm concerned, going for a ride in our car is essential to our mental health."

"Okay," I smiled. "I can support that approach." Still, I did not want to encounter any highway patrol officers. Fortunately, we didn't.

Unfortunately, we never thought about the lack of restrooms that a social closure of this magnitude would impose. By now we'd traveled nearly three hours and had reached the tiny city of South Bend, Washington. I drove one pass down the main drag through town and made a couple of brief excursions through attractive-looking side streets.

At this point, Heidi and I were keenly aware our legs needed stretching and our bladders needed emptying. I recalled seeing an open gas station with a little store about a half mile back on the main road, so I drove there. I went in to inquire about restrooms, and the lone young man on duty curtly informed me none were available.

"Do you know whether anything else is open in town?"

"Nope."

"Thanks," I said, "Good luck to you." I tried to be sensitive to his situation. Maybe his abruptness stemmed from working in a customer vacuum. He could have been fearful we might expose him to COVID if we came into the store.

"Good luck to you, too," he replied, with no emotion or sympathetic look on his face.

"Nothing?" Heidi asked when I got back into the car.

"Nothing. Welcome to the town where my dad was born a hundred and nine years ago. Looks like everything is locked down tight!"

We decided to drive back through the town slowly in case we missed something the first time. Indeed, there was one public toilet which turned out to be unlocked. And uncleaned. It also lacked a supply of the standard paper products. But we made do and decided to return home as quickly as possible. Taking the road heading east across open farmlands toward the interstate highway, we shaved twenty-five miles and thirty minutes off our return journey.

Back in the warmth and safety of our home, we both wondered if the world would ever again be the same. We missed that open, friendly place we had grown up in. Now we found ourselves wistfully remembering and fearful it may not return.

During the following two years, despite the ever-changing rules and regulations about public behavior, from the vaccination lines to the masking arguments, Heidi and I persisted. We went for walks together in our neighborhood and we took a few more road trips. We also spent a lot of time on Zoom with friends around the world, and with those just a few miles away. From my upstairs home office window, I watched the little children who live on our street and thought about how they are being affected, how their parents have been impacted.

I often think about our friends who are schoolteachers, doctors, and frontline workers. I know they have had to cope with the frustrations of their students and families, their patients, their customers. I also know people who have ridden their Pelotons or hiked their way through this pandemic to stay fit. They have avoided other peoples' exhalations and escaped the danger of accidental touch.

I have stayed in my pod with Heidi and have become a cardboard cutout of myself. I watch myself on my monitor. I watch myself listen to other people talking, watch myself give lectures, make comments, respond to questions and sometimes even zone out. Often, as I feel my legs cramping, I wish I could go out for a cup of coffee. On some days, my meetings are back-to-back for hours, and I have no time to even walk across the house to the bathroom.

There are other days when I must remain at the keyboard writing. I am all alone. No one is staring at me. Then I am able to move about the house as I want, but I remain ensconced.

I spend long hours honing words to inform, educate, and change hearts and minds. It's not the same as traveling, but at least I'm not looking at myself on the screen. I only have to see my hands, and look inside my mind or my imagination. These are the best times, along with the other best times: road trips with Heidi.

As restrictions are loosening, and mask requirements are lessening, people are starting to travel more. Organizations are planning to hold conferences in person again. How can they take that risk? Are they pretending there isn't another viral variant on the horizon? One that could still infect and kill people? Maybe not as many...but still leaving some victims with long-COVID symptoms. Or worse, dead before their work was finished, leaving their thoughts unexpressed.

I feel less desirous of adventure that might expose me to disabling illness or premature death. I appreciate not having to travel to meetings or to deliver public lectures because it saves me time and reduces my anxiety about viral contamination to do these activities remotely.

Yet there are times when I am writing, and the words fly through my fingers, and my body feels the motion of the rapid walk through the airport. I hear the rumble of the engines, I feel the pounding of the wheels on the runway, the roar, the lift, the push, and the rising elevation. I know I'm going someplace. I know I'll arrive. I want this kinetic force of life again. I want to walk into an auditorium and feel thousands of eyes upon me. Not just one eye and a bunch of cardboard cutouts. I want to share space, time, and emotions with people whose lives are as rich and complex as my own.

We are beings with feelings and dreams. We need to feel the connections between us. I want that electricity of shared energy, shared emotions, simultaneity, and synchronicity. I'm so blessed to have that on a small scale in my pod with Heidi, and over Zoom through regular communication with our adult children and a few close friends. But I need my motion back, and the space between meetings, between destinations. Instead of responding to deadlines, rarely moving from my desk, I need the space to think, create, and become generative again.

I may have asthma, and I may have a healthy fear of suffocation, but there are many ways to suffocate. I am inoculating myself against sedentary restrictions. I am not going to remain tethered to my computer terminal much longer. It has lulled me into a false sense of security, unsafe for the human spirit. I allowed myself to be swept up in the busy-ness of pandemic panic along with everyone else. We told ourselves because we're busy everything would be fine. We found new ways to remake our world. But the consequences have not been without peril. I am not in motion in a way that brings me in sync with the rhythm of life. I am not in balance. I must recover from this static clinginess, this tailspin. I am determined to breathe deeply and rise again. I can feel it.

Jamison Green is a renowned transgender activist and author of the award-winning memoir/educational and historical text, Becoming a Visible Man (*Vanderbilt University Press, 2020/2004).*

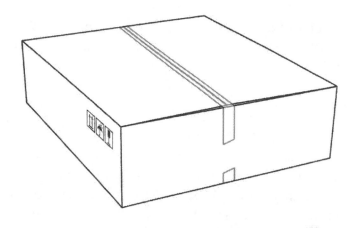

Not My Package

by Weston Anderson

A package arrived one day addressed to a previous occupant of our house. We got a lot of their junk mail, but this was the only package. It was plain brown, sort of medium sized, light weight. We didn't know what to do with it. We put a sticky note on it, "THEY DON'T LIVE HERE," and left it by the door. But the mail carrier wouldn't take it. It sat on our porch for a long time, until I brought it in.

None of us were willing to take it to the post office. The post office wasn't far away but we didn't dare go. This was spring 2020, the start of a pandemic. We didn't go anywhere if it wasn't strictly necessary. Dealing with this package didn't seem necessary. It wasn't worth dying for.

I felt put-upon. The early weeks and months of the pandemic were exhausting and deeply disorienting. I didn't have the capacity to resolve this package thing. It's not my fault it was delivered here, I'd think. I had my mail forwarded, why couldn't they? It's not that hard. I didn't care if this guy received his package or not. I didn't want to expend any effort on this stupid package.

I must not have been alone. My three roommates never did anything with the package either. So it sat in our house, floating from the kitchen counter to the kitchen table, and finally, to a more or less permanent spot by the door. It was out of our way there, mostly.

***

The early days of the pandemic were strange. Within forty-eight hours, me and my three roommates all either lost our jobs or were switched to permanent work-from-home. We went from spending time mostly out of the house to spending time only inside the house. We went from hardly ever seeing each other to seeing no one else. Going nowhere else. We had nothing to do. We weren't trapped, but we were confined.

I started to keep a daily journal.

***

Day 48 of social isolation: "Nothing happens, no one comes, no one goes. It's awful."

***

I was single. My isolation pod consisted of my roommates, and included my best friend, Seth. My roommates and I spent too much time together. We ran out of things to say. It was lonely.

I got tired of seeing that box every time I passed by the door. It was a thing out of place, out of time. It didn't belong. I proposed we open it. I wondered what it could be without actually caring. Opening it just seemed like a way to move forward, to resolve.

Seth was absolutely opposed. Opening the box was a crime. It was an invasion of privacy. It was unethical. Seth was right, of course; but I didn't feel particularly moved by his arguments. Seth was, and is, always challenging me to be better, more conscientious, to tread more lightly. I appreciate (and loathe) a challenge. But I love, admire, and respect Seth. So, I tried to accept his challenges.

I agreed not to open the box.

***

Day 49 of social isolation: I had a vivid dream last night. A boy and I were in bed together. He was around my age. He looked like someone I knew, but wasn't. In the dream, he was slight, light, easily maneuverable. He did what I wanted him to do instinctively. In short, he was a fantasy.

I had this strange sort of exhilarated relief. Like, finally! The boy and I have kissed. We are making out and we have agreed to take things slow. It was so loving and sensual. It felt so good to hold someone like that. To feel loved like that. To feel present like that. It was almost a shame to wake up. But something was wrong. The door of the bedroom kept slipping open. We were trying to make out and be present together, but the door would open, and I would sense a presence in the hallway. There was someone out there.

When I finally got up to investigate, I discovered that the house was filled with people in theatrical dress and stage makeup. I screamed at them to get out of my house, but they just eyed me warily. They didn't budge an inch. I tried all kinds of ways to elicit a response from them. I sprayed them with a hose. I beat them with pillows. I shouted until I was hoarse. None of it made a difference. I couldn't annoy them. I couldn't intimidate them. I felt afraid of them. Their presence unsettled me. If they wanted to, they could overwhelm me. They could hurt me. But they just watched me and looked a little bored and inconvenienced at being made wet.

Then I woke up.

***

I'm a compulsive reader. I've gotten into the habit of reading the news on my phone most mornings. A sure sign that I've become an adult. In the months after the March 2020 lockdowns, there were two stories you could pretty much count on every day:

updated pandemic metrics (how many people tested positive and how many died) and the national toilet paper shortage. I kept track of both every morning, first while drinking coffee and then while sitting on the toilet.

The COVID metrics stories were abstract: graphs of exponential growth, reader friendly explanations of deeply complicated statistical modeling, and ever-growing figures of the dead and the sick.

The toilet paper stories felt more real, somehow. The news ran stories about runs on toilet paper at grocery stores alongside photographs of forlorn shoppers standing in empty paper goods aisles. "Just what am I going to do?" the shoppers seemed to say, slump-shouldered, staring at bare shelves. I'd walked those empty aisles myself, but I never walked the hospital hallways filled with the COVID-sick.

Thank goodness I haven't gotten sick yet, I'd think, *and thank goodness for my bidet.*

By accident, I escaped being a part of either of these stories. I worked from home and was able to self-isolate. My roommates and I stayed healthy in those early months. So, we didn't become part of the statistics reported in the news. Also, shortly before the pandemic hit, Seth and I invested in a bidet and a set of washable microfiber towels. *Butt towels,* we called them. So, we largely avoided the toilet paper shortage.

***

For long periods of time, I'd mostly forget about the box. Most of the time I didn't notice it. But I still had to nudge it out of its corner by the door to sweep up the dust piles, more like dust dunes, that built up around it.

It went on like this for months. I'd forget about the box until it unexpectedly came into view. Whenever I noticed it, I'd go through the entire gamut of emotions I went through when it first arrived. Annoyance that it was delivered at all. Exasperation at the thought of taking it to the post-office. Curiosity about what it may contain. Shame for feeling curious, for wanting to open someone else's mail. Resignation. Acceptance. Forgetfulness.

Then I'd stub my toe on it and it all started up again.

***

Day 118 of social isolation: July. More than halfway through 2020. Cue existential dread. Cue guilt for having wasted another summer of my youth. Cue emotional exhaustion. Cue depression. Cue resentment.

Okay.

Take a sip of coffee. Eat a bite of donut.

***

Oh, how I resented the box. We were in a stalemate. I'd promised not to open it. Throwing it away felt wrong. Taking it to the post office, impossible. There was no way to move forward. The box had become part of the house. It blended in with the new workstation set up in the living room, the flowers I bought when I felt sorry for myself, the stacks of comic books my roommates read, the piles of shoes by the front door.

One day, I looked up and discovered that Seth, my best friend, my creative partner, my housemate, was in the middle of excitedly telling me his plans to move to Vancouver, British Columbia. He wanted to go back to school. I helped him with his application essay. One day I looked up again and Seth had been accepted into an undergraduate program. Seth was moving out, moving on, moving up. I eyed the box in its corner by the door. It hadn't moved more than six inches in six months.

***

Day 268 of social isolation: Time is going by so quickly and soon Seth will be gone. I feel like he and I should do something, many things, while we still can, while it's still so easy.

***

As fast as rounding a corner, Seth moved out; another room-mate moved in. I celebrated the gift of living with a friend and grieved that friend's departure. I forgot about the box.

***

Day 299 of social isolation: Things I miss about Seth. Hearing him laugh, whistle, sing. All the different ways his hair piles on his head. Going on errands together. Grabbing food together. High fives. Riding in his car. The little presents we exchange. His knock on my door. Hugs.

***

Sometime after Seth moved out, the box burst into my con-sciousness again. There it was by the door, as always, at the edge of my peripheral vision. Once again I reminded myself I had prom-ised Seth I wouldn't open it. *But Seth doesn't live here anymore,* my inner voice told me.

That's right. He doesn't live here anymore. So, he doesn't get a say in this anymore. I grabbed the box and fast-walked it to the kitchen table. "I'm opening the box!" I announced to my roommate, who was sitting at his desk in the living room.

"Uh...okay..." he responded.

"Seth doesn't live here anymore!" I said as if that clearly justi-fied the crime I was about to commit. I grabbed a butter knife and sliced through the brown packaging tape that sealed the top of the box. I didn't bother cutting the sides. I slipped my fingers through the top and pried the flaps open with a terrific ripping sound.

I pulled out a handful of packing paper and tossed it aside. I had long suspected that the box might contain a computer component of some kind. Maybe a charging cord or a mouse or something of that nature. I wasn't expecting anything of value. What I relished in that moment was putting the box behind me once and for all and achieving a final resolution to its errant delivery.

When I saw what was inside, I chuckled. I half-screamed at what I saw. I tossed my head back and laughed. My roommate looked at me strangely. "What is it?" he asked. As an answer, I reached inside the box and pulled out what it contained: two rolls of toilet paper.

Weston Anderson (They/Them) is a writer and storyteller living in Portland, OR. They daylight as a science writer in the biomedical research field. Weston spent much of the first two years of the COVID pandemic producing Queer Meets Queer, *a podcast dedicated to telling true LGBTQ+ relationship stories. Weston can be found gardening, hanging out with their dog, and playing dungeons and dragons with their friends.*

Metamorphosis

by Paul Iarrobino

Living through a pandemic has been a roller coaster ride for me. The extreme highs and lows have forced me to make changes and reimagine my life in ways I never thought possible.

My relationship with COVID got off to a rocky start. I was one of the first among my friends to become infected early in the pandemic. I told myself I had the flu. I became weak and lethargic, and much less engaged in my normal routines. Soon, concerned friends started texting me, asking if I had COVID. When I didn't respond, they became more worried and started texting my husband, Arnel. I was given the antigen test when it became available, and it confirmed I had COVID.

My early encounter with COVID reminded me of the five stages of grief: denial, anger, bargaining, depression and acceptance. COVID brought with it a new type of loss: panic and uncertainty I never experienced before.

Denial. Anger. Bargaining. Depression. Each day. Every day. Sometimes all four emotions in one day. Was there Acceptance? Absolutely not.

While in bed scanning my emails, canceled events and volunteer commitments came in one by one. While my hubby seemed to flawlessly adjust to working from home, my schedule was completely gutted, along with my self-employment income stream. I felt increasingly rudderless.

As I gained strength, I wanted to face the world again, but how? As an extrovert, I missed seeing people. That clearly was not an option with COVID. Reality was setting in—there was no more validation from my work or from volunteering in the community. I was no longer needed as a volunteer driver to take older people to the senior center because the senior center was closed. I fell into a big void. I knew if I was struggling, then what were these seniors experiencing? After all, gathering at the center was a major activity in their lives.

A few days later, I invested in a Zoom account. I had very little experience with virtual meetings, but I thought this might pull me out of my slump. I reached out to the local senior center director where I volunteered and pitched the idea of offering a one-time Zoom call with older adults. My thought was a virtual call could help them with this new forced isolation. The director liked the idea, as she was in the process of setting up a Zoom account for the center.

I offered my first Zoom group to a handful of seniors on April 7, 2020. We stumbled through the technology glitches together. "I don't know how to mute." "Can you hear me now?" "How do I turn my camera on?" Our first Zoom meeting was awkward. But the need to meet resonated. Someone asked if we could meet again and that was the beginning of our Tuesday meetings.

I decided to frame the meetings around examining COVID through a lens of gratitude, resilience and connection. There was so much angst initially. This direction helped the group focus and realize this pandemic didn't come with a road map. We needed to support each other and be as flexible as possible.

I found limiting the group to around eight people worked well for the one-hour time block. When this group quickly filled, I started a second, then a third, and a fourth. The overwhelming community need for these remote connections was beyond my bandwidth, but I felt satisfied creating and facilitating these weekly connections.

Being surrounded by so many people, I became fascinated with how they filled the extra time isolating at home by discovering new hobbies or nurturing dormant ones. I became a sponge soaking up ideas. New recipes were popular, and I made my first loaf of bread in my adult life. It was easy to make—a small number of ingredients, a Dutch oven and wax paper and voila.

While in the midst of making this new creation, memories of rolling dough with my mom as a young boy came back. The simple task of baking bread brought me back to special memories of just the two of us in the kitchen while all the older siblings were at school. I felt my mom with me as I kneaded the dough, just like she was more than half a century ago.

I discovered my "COVID convalescent plasma" could help people who were sick and started donating. I learned my first donation helped COVID patients in a North Las Vegas hospital and that was all the reinforcement I needed. I donated a few times until the American Red Cross informed me I didn't have enough COVID antibodies to be helpful. Then, I resumed donating blood as regular donations were down.

My introduction to Ancestry.com started when my friend Jim half-kiddingly challenged us to submit our DNA to see if we were related. This back-and-forth between us went on for months, and it wasn't until the holiday season of 2021 that we did anything about it.

Jim's mother was Italian and sassy like my mom. Jim and I joked over the years that we might have even been distant cousins because our ancestors were all from the Avellino region of Southern Italy. So, here we were: me living in Portland, Oregon, and Jim living in Bellingham, Washington, dripping our saliva into plastic tubes and sending our sputum off in a pre-packaged, secure envelope to a large DNA processing center.

We sent off our samples and eagerly waited about five weeks for our results to arrive. Thanks to Jim's bargain hunting skills, we received a free 90-day subscription to Ancestry.com with our DNA-search purchase. I immediately dove into exploring my family tree.

While I played with Ancestry.com in the past with free seven-day subscriptions, I quickly discovered the website had changed with the times. It was a gold mine of ancestry connections with useful tools. With a multitude of DNA samples being processed during COVID, there was even more scientific evidence linking long-lost relatives and solving family tree puzzles.

My father's maternal and paternal side were easy to trace. In fact, I was able to track both sides of his family to the town of Torre le Nocelle, in the Province of Avellino, back to the 1500's. I started making frequent Internet searches to learn more about my ancestral birthplace. I quickly learned the town's meaning when translating Torre le Nocelle.

First, *Torre* refers to a large tower that early inhabitants built and *Nocelle* is derived from the Latin word *nucella*, which translates to "nuts." Locally, the translation refers to walnuts and filberts (also known as hazelnuts), as they are plentiful there. This immediately started making sense to me because as a kid I remember my dad telling us the translation for our ancestral town was "land of the nuts."

In less than a week, I traced my father's family back 11 generations by not letting one "hint" go unnoticed. I felt proud as I learned more about my roots and about this medieval town with narrow streets, porches, stone arches, and beautiful portals.

Next, I printed off family profiles, photos and historical documents and dropped the package in the mail to my 91-year-old father who lives 3,000 miles away. I knew he would appreciate this historical research. But something unexpected was about to take place. My ancestral gods had a plan of their own.

Despite being from a large family, we are not particularly close. My relationship with my dad and my siblings has been strained most of my life. It is difficult to pinpoint the reasons for our family estrangement.

It has been especially challenging for me to navigate a relationship with my dad for the past ten years, because of the fundamental differences in our social and political ideologies. We see the world very differently. Our contact has always been minimal. We exchange gifts, but only as a formality and nothing more.

Much to my surprise, something changed about a week after my father received the family history packet. Our first phone call lasted about an hour-and-a-half, not the usual awkward three or four minutes. It was as if we both subconsciously knew, if we followed a new ancestral script and dropped the triggering digs, we could forge a new relationship in life.

During that first call, my father filled in some important blanks for me. He supplied me with information about family members who were missing from my newly harvested family tree. I took copious notes, as he spoke so I could go back and research these new clues. My father was pleased with how far my online research had taken me. I kept telling him it really wasn't that difficult since many people before me helped pave the way. As a son though, I valued and appreciated these new personal dynamics between us.

My father began telling me family stories connected to our ancestor's birthplace. I learned about a great uncle who was a high-level military commander. He had been responsible for airlifting life-saving polio vaccines for the children of Torre le Nocelle. My dad told me the townspeople were so grateful, they erected a statue of him in the center of town, as a tribute.

Subsequent calls were filled with family stories I never heard before or was too young to remember. My dad became animated as he made these family members come alive for me. Our conversations sparked a part of him that was dormant for decades, a part of him that craved reactivation. He became more gregarious and funny. He became the father I haven't experienced in several decades.

It wasn't long before my father took me under his wing and directed me to family members all over the world to help fill in the blanks. These were relatives from the US and abroad I never knew existed. They included a ninety-year-old great uncle who is a retired monk living in California and a cousin from Torre le Nocelle, who now lives in Switzerland. That cousin only speaks Italian, but thanks to Google Translate, a whole new relationship is developing as we learn about each other.

More recently, I connected with a second cousin who is an artist living in Santa Fe. I will be traveling to New Mexico for business in a few months. My husband, Arnel, and I will meet him in person for the first time. Through our email exchanges, he has shared a lot of family history I never knew.

As mask mandates lift and scientific advances are made, I have a strong desire to take an ancestral journey to Torre le Nocelle. I want to experience this ancient village full of my family's history for myself.

Despite the havoc the pandemic unleashed, it also brought me new possibilities. Yes, I got off to a rough start with COVID, but as I leaned into the extra time isolating at home provided, my heart opened to new discoveries. The best one has been the new relationship I began with my father, and it continues today. This life changing experience is something I never imagined possible before COVID.

Paul credits his upbringing in a large, Italian, East Coast family for helping him speak up at the dining room table, lest he go unheard. Having lived in Portland, Oregon, for over 30 years, he enjoys performing, producing shows, creating documentaries, teaching, and coaching. Paul has appeared in numerous national storytelling productions. You can follow Paul at www.ourboldvoices.com.

Shelter in Place 2020

by Randa Cleaves Abramson

In My Circle: 19

I bear witness to the strolling mother
    her two-year-old in bright ducky boots
    waving to all he sees
Her youngest swaddled to her chest
    clinging to an uncertain future

I bear witness to the neighbor
    walking his wiggly dog
    wife stranded in Asia
Using furry companionship as a shield against
    the perils of the world

I bear witness to the ER nurse, my neighbor
    who cried for hours yesterday
    face and emotions unmasked
Despondent because
    patients scream
        and
they don't even cover dead bodies anymore

I bear witness to the three-year-old

careening around his house
stuck inside because
         there are bugs outside
Mom and Dad at the limits of what they can provide
    and what they can endure

I bear witness to my friend back east
        who answers the phone and hears
        She is dead, He is sick
Because he knows the cause
        he stumbles into walls

I bear witness to the long-married couple
        now sheltering countryside
        suddenly isolated from others
Now re-discovering their love
away from demands of calendars

I bear witness to the citizen
        recently released from prison
        new job and hope obliterated
Struggling to resist catapulting back to old patterns
        while the world crashes down around him

I bear witness to a political candidate
        brave enough to take a stand
        trying to be heard
Wanting to repair the rifts
        willing to take on the despair

I bear witness to singers, actors, and musicians
        without a stage
        without an audience
Trapped in solitude
        souls silenced

I bear witness to workers who show up
        and stock shelves
        and bravely ring us up
Wondering if their recompense will be
        more than a paycheck; a disease

I bear witness to my fears
    vulnerable age
    vulnerable lungs
I write and contemplate
    and bear witness to the suffering of others

Tie a Yellow Ribbon

Poetry succumbed to the virus
  Yellow ribbons
    symbol of binding ties to a loved one in combat or jail
     became portrayal of pandemic prison
      haphazardly encircling playgrounds
       squelching climbing and circling and sliding and do it again
                            do it again

Poetry surrendered to politics
  Yellow tape of police lines overpowered oak trees
    voices crying out for justice usurped lyrics
     din and mayhem overpowered melody
      violence overshadowed reunions

How long do ribbons endure?
  oak trees grow
    circumferences change
     ribbons rot
      symbols saturate and
       succumb

Shelter in place Act Two

Do you know anyone who's had it?
Tallies of cases and deaths rise daily
Separately we survive month after month
Together in our Isolation

I can't breathe
Began as a plea from one suffocating man
Competed with COVID to infect thousands
      a battle cry for reform
      echoed by millions as the smoke from infernos
      choked the protesting states
      amplifying injustice

Stay inside
We sheltered in place, stayed inside
      to be safe from the microscopic threat
But outdoors was safe
      except for children's playgrounds
Now lands where adults and families play are off limits
      from the larger danger of conflagration

When will we?
Linger in a restaurant
Watch a child board a school bus
Sit as live audience for performers
Embrace friends
Fly to celebrate with family
Mourn together those we've lost

Randa has written many words to raise funds for nonprofit organizations during her forty plus year career, but it took relocating to the northwest from New Jersey decades ago to start to write poetry. First the mountains and landscapes of Washington provided inspiration and living in Oregon since 2010 provided the stimulation to keep writing. She was drawn to share her works when she read a notice about the Pacific Wonderland Poets Group at the Beaverton Library. During the months of the pandemic, the weekly zoom sessions became a lifeline for its stalwart eight members to safely share thoughts and fears about the emotional times we were living through. These three poems were written between May and September of 2020.

3,000 Square Feet

by Holly Robison

3,000 square feet—not a mansion, but plenty of room for my family of six. Suddenly COVID arrived and our lives were turned upside down. In the spring of 2020, we were asked to stay home and our family experienced new extremes. I used to wake up early every weekday, making my family breakfast, and helping with last minute projects and assignments before sending them all out the door to school and work. I was left with a quiet house all to myself to clean, to create, to enjoy friends and to fulfill my service obligations. Suddenly we had too much free time, too much constant family interaction, too much anxiety, too little structure, too little outside stimulation, too little physical interaction.

Here's a typical scene:

Eli (10) entered his imaginary world. Bang! Racing back and forth from one room to the other, he exploded onto the couch in some invisible battle. Clash! Crash! He swung his arms this way and that. No one could see his foes, but no one could concentrate on anything else!

Audrey (17) lay on the couch with an elephant pillow over her head. She tried to shake her constant anxiety headache and stay present at the same time. Every time Eli ran by, she cringed.

Nora (15) sat in the corner meticulously placing tiny, sparkly diamonds on her current diamond art piece. She was trying to listen to her audiobook, but Eli's battle kept creeping in. In her "I'm trying not to kill you" voice, she kept reminding him that he needed to stop. He responded with his classic whine.

John (my husband) sat at the other end of the table working on a puzzle. His system was to painstakingly organize each piece by placing them in rows by shape. He was tempted to give the evil eye to anyone who offered an unwanted helping hand.

Collier (13) was in the kitchen doing his new "I'm bored" activity: baking. Every time Eli ran into the kitchen area, Collier yelled at him to get out, adding his voice to the cacophony.

I couldn't feel settled. I wanted to be active in what my family was doing. I wanted to calm the chaos, but I couldn't figure out how. I couldn't focus on a project of my own when the mood of the home was in turmoil.

Every day we were stepping on each other's toes in various ways. It wasn't always Eli causing the contention. Everyone took their turn. As Mom, I wondered what I'd done wrong. Aren't moms supposed to be able to solve any problem, cure any ailment? That was the kind of mom I wanted to be, even if it was untrue and unrealistic. I felt I was failing! The six of us lived in the same house, as a family, yet it seemed that everyone preferred to keep to themselves. We were working on our forever family but under the circumstances forever felt like an awfully long time.

I wanted something different. John and I wanted something different. So together we took it to God. We asked for a way to bring more peace to our home.

As is so often the case, the answer we got wasn't what we expected: daily planned family activities with technology-free time. Can you just imagine how that was received in our family council? "Mom, we are together ALL the time! You want to plan more time together!? Please, no!" "You've got to be kidding me! Don't you think this quarantine is enough torture?" "I don't want to!"—with extra whine. "Can we watch a movie every day for our family activity?" "I'm not putting my phone away! What good will that do!"

My one cheerleader and co-conspirator was John. He proclaimed, "It will be fun! And you are going to like it!" with great conviction.

Our plan was to each take turns planning one family activity everyday where everyone would put phones away and do something together. I gave examples: "We could do an art project, a baking contest, play a game, go for a walk or hike, make plans for a service project." I saw that the possibilities were endless. My children saw endless torture!

And so it began. Monday at breakfast I told everyone to meet at the kitchen table at 4 o'clock for our first family activity. Phones would go on the counter. Everyone was encouraged to bring their creativity. To prepare, I gathered all the cardboard and cereal boxes from the recycling bin. I added leaves to extend the table and covered it with a plastic tablecloth. I got out construction paper, acrylic paints, markers, scissors, box cutters and cutting boards. I wanted everyone to have supplies at their fingertips for anything their imagination might create. I found examples of a Picasso inspired face mask project that I planned to show the family.

At the appointed time, everyone gathered with minor arm pulling. We only had to call for Nora and Collier twice! Audrey and Nora tried to pretend like they forgot about the putting phones away part. But I said, "Phones go on the counter for the next two hours." With huffs and puffs they put them away. Then they insisted, "Mom and Dad, you too!" Of course, of course!

I explained the plan, showed them the examples, and set everyone loose with the supplies. There was some grumbling, "I can't think of anything!" and "I can't do this!" With encouragement and a little patience, it turned out just as I imagined. We were each in our zone, cutting, coloring, placing, gluing, and imagining. The completed masks hung on our front door for months. We pointed out things that we liked, "I like how Eli made two opposite masks." "It's cool how Audrey has so many different textures." "Collier's mask looks evil, cool!" There was a lot to clean up, but it was all worth it.

Over the course of the next few months, we did a plethora of phone-free activities. It felt like we entered the Twilight Zone when every day we got the same reluctant responses to the expected recurring event. But we persevered, poor attitudes and all, and we noticed a difference. More peace, less contention. More cooperation, less complaining.

Audrey taught us a TikTok dance. Even John participated, making all of us laugh. Collier conducted a baking competition that ended with a collection of desserts for dinner. John planned a Silver Falls hike that we completed, in spite of the wet weather. Nora had us all sit and listen to a beloved audiobook and work on diamond art. Eli had us play around the world Ping-Pong that almost ended in a pile up. We played Pictionary drawing on each other's backs. We even made concessions by having a movie marathon as one of our family activities. (I have literally months of family activity ideas if you are interested!)

John was out of the mix sometimes. Whereas many dads were working from home, if they still had jobs, Nurse Practitioners do not have that option. So every other week John would spend his days at the hospital where he had new COVID safety protocols. We worried about him from home. Then it was up to me and the kids to carry on with our daily family phone-free activities. We got a system down.

Feeling like we'd made it over the hurdle of connecting and getting along as a family, it was time to tackle the next one. Spring had passed and summer was drawing to a close. What to do about school? No one wanted to relive the online instruction that public school had provided in the Spring. As a family we prayed about what to do. We felt inspired to make a change. After 12 years of being a part of the public school system, we ventured out on our own and became a homeschool family. This change brought so many new opportunities, new mentors and new friends. Eli started reading books on Zoom with his grandma. We connected with cousins in Florida to conduct science experiments and read and discuss history. Audrey and Nora took the same online college classes, studying together for the first time. Collier and I read *Uncle Tom's*

Cabin. Our dinner topics revolved around what everyone was learning more than ever before. We were connecting in new ways through education.

When the schools opened back up in Oregon for in-person learning and much of our community was going back to school, our life didn't change. We were still a family that stayed home together and learned together. That is the biggest change that COVID brought to our family. In March of 2020 everything shut down and everyone stayed home, and that is where we've stayed. Yes, our children are involved in sports and other social activities in the afternoon and evenings. But I'm almost never home alone. We never went back to just sending everyone out the door in the morning and coming back together in the evening.

As time passed, our daily planned family-phone-free activities fell by the wayside to other priorities. More extracurriculars opened up and I found myself playing chauffeur more and more. I felt that same nagging feeling that something needed to change. The interesting thing is that now the family wasn't spending enough time together. I find myself asking us to set aside one night a week for a planned family activity. We aren't as crazy or intense as we were in 2020 but we get out a game or we grab some paper and play a drawing game because we like spending time together. COVID helped us realize that.

Two years in, homeschooling works well for us. Audrey graduated with a year of college under her belt and is off serving a mission in Brazil, proving that we raised a well-adjusted, 'I can handle anything' young lady. (I know I really can't take much credit.) Nora is graduating this year from high school with an associate degree and looking to a bright future at OSU (Oregon State University). Collier learned some lessons the hard way, but developed enough self-discipline to try his hand at community college classes as a sophomore. He has impressed us all. While John and I thought Eli would be one of the hardest to homeschool, he's proved otherwise. This year he is studying the founding of our nation. He is dissecting the constitution, setting his own pace and getting it done.

Both he and I have a greater appreciation for our founding fathers. Having read so many books about them, they feel like friends.

A typical day around here lately is:

Eli, in his comfy robe, sits at the kitchen table with his books and laptop.

Collier sprawled on the floor of the playroom with papers and books strewn around him. He calls out to Nora in her room so they can talk about the classes they are taking together.

John and I bounce around from kids' projects to our own projects. We think of Audrey on her adventure in Brazil.

We come together for most of our meals. It feels good. Don't get me wrong, we all have our moments of hiding in our room for some alone time. But COVID sent us home and we stayed. Now I wouldn't have it any other way! 3,000 square feet is just right. I don't wonder what I did wrong anymore. I look at our family and I see what we did right!

Holly Robison is a storyteller, musician, presenter, mentor and—first and foremost—a wife and mother. She's been sharing stories of folklore and history for 20 years and has connected with audiences all over the world. Holly received her BA in Theater from Brigham Young University. Her passion is helping youth find their voice through Storytelling. She founded the Murray, UT, and Hillsboro, OR, Storytelling Festivals. Holly offers workshops in beginning storytelling, nature stories, crafting family and history stories and body language.

It Started with a Walk...

by Michael Coscia

As Auld Lang Syne was preparing to bid farewell to a not-so-great 2019, I had just finished working a film production office job with some of the most unprofessional people I'd ever met. Whenever my boss was about to lie to me, and she often did, she'd nervously twirl her blond hair between her fingers while offering niceties that were as thin as her integrity.

That woman was the final straw in a series of job-related disappointments. I foolishly believed that working hard and doing good work came with appreciation from co-workers, especially bosses. I was wrong.

In retrospect I should have quit. My years of experience and vast knowledge were not being appreciated. Because I grew up believing quitting was a sign of weakness, I plowed through and honored my personal commitment to stay with the project to its end. I was determined not to let them, or myself, see me as weak.

I dreaded going to work every morning. I white-knuckled the steering wheel as I drove the congested freeway, certain the other drivers were feeling the same about their jobs. I quietly vowed to make a drastic change in the new year, to focus on me and what made me happy.

I knew that being creative made me happy. I knew that writing made me happy.

But at that time, I was not happy, even after the job ended. There was an aching fear of taking that first step to personal independence. I was trapped by too much indecision and not enough confidence. I was at a career and personal dead-end, a mid-life crisis that seemed insurmountable.

Little did I know upcoming events would take me on a roller-coaster journey of self-discovery.

It was early March 2020, just before covid became COVID, when I took a walk in the neighborhood. The idea of wearing a mask was not yet in our consciousness though there were warnings about not gathering in large groups. The news was ominous, but a lot of people were assuming "it's not going to happen to me," including me. We had no idea what was soon to wreak havoc upon us and decimate life as we knew it.

So, there I was soaking up the Southern California sunshine, enjoying the neighborhood vibes, and minding my own business, when I ran into a woman I'd seen before, though we'd never met. She was walking her dog, and with her, I assumed, was her daughter. The young girl looked about eight years old.

We exchanged neighborly hellos, and then the girl beelined towards me, invading my personal space with complete abandon. I thought she was about to hug my thigh. I tensed up.

Instead, the little girl held out her hand and offered me a pinecone, placing it in the palm of my hand. She smiled that bright smile only a child knows and, without uttering a single word, hurried back to hide behind her mother.

I was stunned and didn't know quite what to do. The mother was beaming. The young girl was beaming. So, I did the gentlemanly thing and beamed right back at them. Inside I was uncomfortable and wondering what just happened.

I thanked her, said goodbye, and hurried on my way. The pine-cone was oozing sap in the palm of my hand, and its stickiness was making my palm itchy.

As I turned the corner, I wanted to throw it away. But just when I was about to toss it, the pinecone seemed to be glued to my palm refusing to budge, wanting me to keep it, to carry it with me for the rest of my walk.

As I neared home, I once again tried tossing the pinecone into the bushes, but again, it wouldn't let me. So, I brought the pine-cone inside and placed it on the kitchen counter.

Over the next couple of weeks, COVID hit hard, and the news was scary. We were hunkering down from an unknown force we didn't understand...the numbers of infections and people hospital-ized kept rising...day after day...the worry...the deaths...the fear...I watched the news and constantly checked the COVID numbers for Los Angeles, refreshing websites too many times to count.

The intense anxiety from being alone combined with the abso-lute boredom from being locked inside my small apartment began to take its toll on me. I was obsessed with COVID, and it wasn't good for my mental health. I had to force myself away from the overwhelming COVID news refresh.

I now had a choice. I could waste hours binging on Netflix or playing Internet Solitaire, or I could do something...but what?

Tick, tock, tick, tock. Day into night into day all seemed like a blur. I often asked myself what day it was. Was it Monday? Was it Friday? Or worse, what month?

The sticky pinecone was still on the kitchen counter and every day when I looked at it, I kept seeing the little girl's beaming face. I often laughed thinking it had some kind of magical power over me. I just couldn't throw it away, so there it stayed on my kitchen counter.

The COVID loneliness and fear were paralyzing. People I knew were sick and people I knew had died. Every telephone conversation began with a tentative fear-tinged, "How are you feeling?" followed by a deep sigh of relief when the person said they were doing fine.

I wasn't showering daily. I wasn't shaving. I was drinking way too much coffee. I was baking desserts and eating way too much sugar. I guess I could say I was trying to eat my way out of loneliness. It wasn't working.

One morning as I stumbled into the bathroom, I looked in the mirror and was shocked at what I saw. My hair was much longer and unruly, and my usually clean-shaven face hadn't been shaved in weeks. I was seeing a stranger, but I knew he had to be me. I was the only one living in my apartment.

"Who are you?" I whispered.

No answer.

I ran my fingers along my mirrored face for a familiar feeling. I felt nothing.

Who was this man staring back at me? Was he just me in a lazy unkempt disguise or was this mirror image trying to tell me something? I needed to find out, but how?

Coincidentally, or not so coincidentally, I'd been listening to various podcasts and found myself clicking on a self-help podcast where the host was raving about a newly published best-selling self-help book about discovering one's true self. My curiosity was piqued and without a second thought, I logged onto Amazon and purchased the book.

Over the next week, I read that book cover to cover and did all the suggested assignments. I was astounded at all the layers I peeled away in order to get to my core, to get to know me. There were tears. There were aha moments. There was frustration. There were hints of joy. It wasn't easy, but somehow, I got through it. I was discovering my one true self, and I was slowly, very slowly, beginning to admire the man I was discovering. He was strong. He was confident. He was the opposite of the person I'd been just months earlier. He was the new me.

While making all the inroads into self-discovery, the pinecone continued to sit on my counter. It was now taking on an importance in my life, yet I still didn't know for what purpose. I found its presence calming and it kept bringing me back to that moment when the beaming little girl so generously offered it to me.

Shortly thereafter, I was masked and on my daily walk through the neighborhood when I saw the girl's mother walking her dog. I hurried towards her and told her the story of her daughter giving me the sticky pinecone. She remembered it clearly. I explained how the pinecone was sitting on my kitchen counter.

The woman told me that her daughter never gravitates towards people, but for some reason that day, her little girl felt a connection with me and wanted to share. I must've looked confused because she then asked, "You don't know, do you?" I hadn't a clue.

Fighting back a tear or two, she told me her daughter's autistic.

There was a moment of silence where neither of us knew what to say next. And in that silence, I had a small yet huge aha moment when I suddenly understood that the little pinecone was more than just a pinecone.

I told the woman to thank her daughter and to tell her I still had her gift. She assured me her daughter would be thrilled to hear it.

By the time I got home, my heart was overflowing with emotion.

That little girl saw something in me, maybe the damaged part of me. She offered the gift of unconditional kindness, of acceptance. Her simple gesture cracked the protective wall I'd built around myself and hid behind, giving me a glimpse of something new, a sliver of hope that refused to be ignored. It started me on the journey of self-reconciliation.

I knew I had to share the pinecone story, and I did, by writing it and posting it on my blog.

The following day, a director friend who read the blog sent me a note saying he loved the story, suggesting it should be turned into a short film. It was an opportunity I couldn't refuse, and that afternoon I wrote the script. It flowed out of me as if I was living it again... not only the words but the essence of kindness.

A few months later we shot the film.

I'm happy to say the resulting short film, Sticky Pinecones, resonated with a lot of people, even winning a couple of awards at a film festival. It has initiated conversations about kindness and acceptance and human nature and autism.

I often think about the pre-COVID-quarantine me and the post-COVID-quarantine me and I see very few similarities. It's like that pre-quarantine me is someone I used to know, someone who desperately needed to be awakened, someone who needed permission to leave the past behind and live in the moment, to be present in who I am.

We don't always know each other's story. A little gesture of kindness, like giving someone a pinecone, can ignite a dormant part of us and inspire us to grow. So now whenever I take my walks, I make sure to say hello to the people I pass. It's my way of letting them know I see them, I acknowledge them, and they are not invisible.

It's been interesting to see how people react... some with surprise... some with apprehension... some ignore me... and then there are those whose eyes light up offering a return smile and a few friendly words.

Some of the people I see are neighbors who've lived around me for years who've never acknowledged me before, but after my making the effort, they now say hello.

And yes, I still have the pinecone.

It's carefully wrapped in plastic and tucked away in my memory box where I keep souvenirs of life's beautiful moments.

And to think, it all started with a walk....

Michael Coscia is a filmmaker, writer, and storyteller.

His short film, Sticky Pinecones, *has been an official selection in multiple film festivals winning Best Message in a Short Film and a Producer's Choice Award.*

When he's not writing scripts or essays, he can be heard telling his stories at Strong Words, Voices of the City, *a monthly storytelling event.*

He treasures a good book, a glass of wine, and a good song... sometimes all at the same time.

Michael currently lives in Los Angeles where he continues to unsuccessfully grow basil.

A Long COVID Journey

by Brenda Culhane

It didn't feel like a big deal. It was just a sore throat and a slight fever. So, I called my doctor to get her advice. The date was March 14, 2020. She wasn't too concerned but referred me to triage to rule out the possibility of COVID. Shortly thereafter, a nurse called and asked me thousands of questions. After 45 minutes he said, "You may be at moderate risk for COVID, so I want you to come in and have a test." I thought they were both overreacting, but I followed through. When I arrived at the doctor's office, there was no one in the waiting room. I was told to sit in a corner of the waiting room and wait for someone to come and get me. The intake receptionist looked very frightened of me.

A medical assistant finally called me into an exam room. On the way to the exam room, all of the personnel were staring at me from the far end of the room. Just like the receptionist, they all looked frightened, too. The doctor acknowledged that she had never given a COVID test before. She wore a mask, a face shield, rubber gloves, and paper protection covering her body and shoes. Due to all the gear she wore, she had problems navigating the equipment and had to get assistance several times. She was hesitant and had to try a few times before she was able to get a nasal swab sample. Getting the nasal swab sample was painful and it felt like the doctor was pushing the swab right up into my brain. She told me they would call with the results in a couple days. As I left the exam room, I saw the same people staring and still keeping their distance from me.

As it turns out, my test was positive. I immediately called everyone that I had been in contact with over the past seven days and advised them to get tested. I felt horrible that I had exposed my friends to this frightening disease. Fortunately, I had infected no one.

I told my neighbors and word spread like wildfire. I was quarantined and spent a lot of time looking out my front window. People out walking in my neighborhood would cross the street when they came near my house. It was a lonely and difficult time for me. My doctor called me daily. I progressively got worse, and the doctor decided it was time for me to go to the hospital. I was terrified. I quickly made agreements to leave my home and a friend agreed to care of my dog, Emmy.

I knew Italy ran out of beds and had to put their COVID patients in tents on the hospital grounds. In the ambulance, I asked the attendant if I was going to be put in a tent and he laughed. I didn't think it was funny. He reassured me that there was a room waiting for me.

My seven-day hospital stay is a blur in my mind. All the nurses looked like Martians in their protective garb. They explained that it took them 15-20 minutes to gear up and the same amount of time to disinfect themselves after leaving my room. I tried not to take it personally, but they were disinfecting themselves because of ME! I had a bad sore throat, a fever, and a headache. My brain fog made it difficult to understand much of anything and I was unable to speak most of the time. Due to severe night sweats, my sheets were changed daily.

After 7 days in the hospital, I was released to go home. I wanted to go into a care facility because I couldn't even walk to the kitchen or stand up long enough to cook for myself. Test kits weren't available and, as a result, I couldn't prove that I no longer had COVID. No facility wanted to take in a COVID patient.

Leaving the hospital in a wheelchair was an incredible experience. Before I was wheeled out, all the hallways had to be cleared of people. When I left the elevator, large groups of people stood 20 feet away waiting for the COVID patient to pass. Some looked curious, but most looked frightened.

At last, I was home and reunited with Emmy. I missed my loyal canine companion. A friend organized an online meal train and people brought food for me every day. People I didn't even know signed up to bring food. I was so touched by their thoughtfulness. They left the food on the porch, rang the doorbell and immediately left. They would stand out in the street as I waved a gesture of thanks for my wonderful care packages. I have never felt such love in my life. My neighbors checked on me daily and went food shopping for me. A friend came every day for months to walk my dog.

Although my mind was hazy during my first weeks back home, some things did stand out. A nurse, a physical therapist, an occupational therapist, and a social worker came to my home weekly. The nurse was the first to arrive and I watched as she spent about 20 minutes on my porch spraying herself down and putting on protective clothing, mask, shields etc. I opened the door for her, then I immediately stepped about 15 feet away from her and sat on my couch. Of course, I was masked. I really liked her and trusted her, but it felt strange to have someone in my home. When she left, she spent another 20 minutes changing, spraying and waving things in the air. It was most interesting to watch. After that, all of my medical appointments were on Zoom. Since a COVID test wasn't available to me at that time, I was unable to get a negative-confirming COVID test to prove that I no longer had COVID.

Upon checking with my doctor, she told me that since I'd been out of the hospital for 2 weeks and I no longer had symptoms, the CDC finally decided I was officially COVID-free. I received this information from my doctor almost 5 weeks after I left the hospital!

It is frustrating to think during all that time I had been treated as if I had active COVID. At that point, healthcare people were allowed into my home. They all sat across the room, and they all sat far from me. One thing that stands out for me is when the physical therapist sat down on my couch next to me and felt my pulse. I almost swooned! I hadn't been touched in several months and I fought back my tears. She wasn't afraid of me, and she touched me! I will remember that moment for the rest of my life.

After that experience, I was able to go for very short walks with my physical therapist. Initially, all I could do was walk down the five steps from my porch to the sidewalk. Each week I could walk a little further. Any kind of physical activity exhausted me. Some days I was not able to walk at all.

After about 3 months, my medical team decided I no longer needed home health care. I then began my own walking ritual. My goal was to walk around the block, and it took me several months to accomplish that goal. I remember the day I finally did it! I was so happy! I kept moving towards the goals that were set for me.

There were some victories, but there were many more setbacks. I learned to let go of my expectations. I had to change my definition of success. I learned to set small goals for myself and to accept those smaller goals. I learned to ask for help. I learned that setbacks are a normal part of recovery and I no longer got upset when setbacks occurred. I learned that many people loved me and that they were there to support me. I learned that I am a strong woman! I also cried a lot.

Today my life is very different. I still struggle with brain fog. That means I get lost when I'm driving, that I constantly forget what I'm doing, and that I miss meetings. I sometimes forget where I put things, and that I often can't find words when I'm trying to talk. I also forget to pay bills, and that if something has more than two parts to it I struggle to understand it. I really worry that I have dementia.

I have totally reworked my life because some days I have no energy at all. I try to do things in the morning because by 2 o'clock I run out of energy. Some days, I'm unable to get out of the house at all. About six months ago, I began feeling more energetic and was able to do more on good days.

I experienced a lot of dizziness for months. At home, when the dizziness is intense, I bump into walls and need to steady myself to get around the house. Sometimes I experience double vision. I've adapted to it, but I still get dizzy, and it really is a challenge to go places.

After living with long-COVID for about six months, I experienced an elevated heart rate that sent me to the emergency room. I was diagnosed with atrial fibrillation, and they finally ended up using those paddles on me to regulate my heart. I had a healthy heart all my life, so COVID was suspected as being the cause. I now am on blood thinners for the rest of my life.

I have received other new diagnoses since contracting COVID. I struggle with chronic fatigue syndrome. Although I do not have a traumatic brain injury, I am being treated as if I do based on my symptoms. All caused by COVID. I feel like the virus is still inside me and it is trying to kill me.

I'm trying to make peace with COVID. We have been together for over two years now. I'm very grateful for what I've overcome, but still resent how small my life has become.

One of my biggest disappointments is that it took so long for the medical community to acknowledge our collective symptoms needed specific medical intervention. When I finally met with the specialist online, she really had no answers for me. Because COVID and Long COVID are so new to the medical community and have only recently been acknowledged, many of my questions remain unanswered. Everything she suggested to me I was already doing. I attended a Long COVID group and that turned out to be very helpful. The COVID specialists are still learning and we are their teachers. The East Coast is further ahead than the West

Coast and they are sharing what they have learned. I have recently been referred to an intervention developed in England to help COVID "long-haulers." This field is still new and countries all over the world are learning from each other.

I still suffer from Long COVID, but all the struggles have taught me to see things in new ways. Now, when I see my dog sleeping on the couch or when I see a richly colored flower or a sunset, I pay attention. When I see two older people walking down the street holding hands, or when I see something beautiful, I get this tickling feeling in my solar plexus that shoots up and down. It is such a deep feeling of joy that is hard to explain. It's so intense that it's almost painful. I have never felt that magnitude or that depth of feeling before. I feel like I'm floating above my body. I have read that when someone feels deep pain, they also feel its opposite: great joy. This joy is offered to us, and it is ours if we can grab it. I think the offer is there for me, and so is the chance to make my life fuller and more complete. The painful experiences somehow balance my challenges. It's like the light at the end of the storm. My hope is that maybe, just maybe, my life will expand enough to include more joy. All I need to do is grab it.

Brenda has been struggling with long COVID for over two years. Because of exhaustion and brain fog, she found it necessary to let go of the majority of her activities. What remains are those activities she loves best...playing ukulele, harmonica, and spoons. She entertains groups as a ventriloquist with her yodeling dog Charlotte and her real dog Emmy is her constant companion. She is 81 years young and lives in Portland.

Love in the Time of COVID

by Shere Coleman

A journey of loving, longing,
returning often to my own heart's
carriage room where I search for
a time-travel vehicle,
with a full tank for a voyage
sometimes a half-world away.

Bodies I cannot press against,
hair I cannot bury my nose in
vocals I cannot tune to,
those who taught me long ago,
love isn't bounded by distance.

Without tech tools of the day
could I honestly say
I can conjure sounds, faces,
and fill in the rest?
Yes I say, in wonder, tuning to
tone and pattern and pacing.

Alone, confined, the questions,
disappointments, confusion,
all press, point, direct, suggest.
I listen to the chorus of the heart
chamber's music rhythm and beat
yearning to dance and laugh
longing for happy feet.

Astronaut of the inner cosmos,
snap an inner space snapshot
find a pocketed place
to land my own rocket
and take an inner space walk
on the dark side.

Ground control calls me back.
Back to the earth under my feet
the pleasures and wonder of creation
and created, and I ask,
how much, at what cost?

Follow fine threads, ride word waves
and never abandon Together,
For love is a wild creature, teacher.
Reach in and out of the abyss of silence
find a lake a stream or ocean to wash
the needs of ourselves or each other.

This is it, why swimming soothes
inner streams, quiets a rage
a drought or a flood.
Swim through rapids
and eddy's
observe the shore,
her rocks and flora
until a bank beckons,
it will,
I reckon.

Shere Coleman is a lifelong working, exhibiting, and teaching artist. She has been an oral storyteller in the schools, a writer/presenter of historical characters with Aspen Historical Society, a TEDx presenter. She holds a BFA Painting from Pacific Northwest College of Art, and an MAEd in Curriculum and Instruction. She is a contributing poet in the 2021 anthology Opening the Gate. *Shere will cross oceans and continents in search of puppet masters and mythologists.*

"Through the act of making, my world is vibrant, connections are formed, and I learn and love."

The Healing Wisdom of Ancient Trees and Core Values

by Judith Ashley

I am an Immortal Soul inhabiting an Ancient Tree.

These nine words, the beginning of meditation *Energy One* by Colette Baron-Reid, resonated with me the first time I heard them. I've spent hours listening to the meditation and pondering why.

What I find fascinating is I'd listened to that meditation a number of times before I heard the full first line, all nine words!

Initially all I heard was *I am an Ancient Tree.*

From July 30, 2020, until today, those nine words are my touchstone. They comfort me even now and were a lifeline to sanity during the dark days of 2021.

There are phrases and concepts I know by heart. Every time I listen to the whole recording or even remember one piece of it, I am uplifted. My perception of being isolated, alone, uncertain does not have to be my truth.

What can be my truth? What did I draw upon during those dark days, weeks, and months of 2021?

I am an Immortal Soul inhabiting an Ancient Tree. I have a right to be here.

I remember listening to the Lt. Gov. of Texas saying that grandparents were willing to die in order for the businesses to stay open without any masking precautions, physical distancing, etc. Well, he got my attention! Who was he to say I would rather die than wear a mask and keep physical distance? After taking a deep breath, I sent a prayer of gratitude that I did not live in Texas or any other state that thought I was expendable, of less importance than a business.

I am an Immortal Soul inhabiting an Ancient Tree. My roots grow deeper than I am tall.

When I look back over the decades, I look for the gifts in the crippling challenges I've overcome. Those challenges have provided me with a wealth of life experiences upon which to draw. And while I've never lived through a pandemic before, unless you consider polio a pandemic, I have lived through domestic violence, divorce, single parenting, cancer and acquired brain injuries.

How does this fit with being *an immortal soul inhabiting an ancient tree?*

Ancient trees become ancient because they take nourishment from the soil, from what has decayed, from what was left behind. They can take what they need to sustain themselves, to grow taller, stronger. Trees, ancient trees especially are wise. They do not take into themselves that which does not serve them.

The roots of trees grow deep and also outward in all directions. An ancient tree's roots are deeper than it is tall. Roots cover an amazing amount of land, intertwining with other trees' roots. Being interconnected creates a strong web of support. It's been years and yet I still remember walking in an old growth forest, feeling my world shift as I was enveloped by the vibes, the energy of certainty.

However, for a time during the pandemic, I was not listening to this meditation, and I was not reminding myself of this message. I forgot I am energetically connected to the world around me. The few friends I have were also struggling. My world had diminished. Going to the store for groceries was beyond my ability, not physically, but the fear of the COVID Virus had shrunk my world to my small house and a walk around the block. Of course, I wore a mask, kept physical distance, and then sanitized hands, shoes, etc. when I got home.

Several months passed before I began to control the fear and contemplate moving forward with my life. I finally remembered to ask myself key questions:

How was this fear serving me?

What did I need to create a better life for myself?

I believe in "life lessons." Life lessons are the gifts we receive from life events, especially the ones that are difficult, the ones we don't want to experience.

I knew there was a gift somewhere in this experience but where it was and what it was? No easy or immediate answers. And while in the moment, I haven't always found the gift, as time has passed, I have always found at least one blessing if not many.

I am an Ancient tree my roots are deeper than I am tall. How to find those gifts I believed were there so I could take what served me and leave the rest behind.

Colette Baron-Reid decided to hold her virtual event again in 2021. Seeing the invitation to attend, reminded me that I had stopped listening to the meditation and also stopped my spiritual practices. Actually, that is only half-true. I still held my Gratitude Stone at the end of each day and said some words about something for which I was grateful, but *I* wasn't invested in the practice. I was just repeating my practice by rote without thought or emotions.

I listened again to this meditation, was reminded that my roots were deep and spread outward. I was connected energetically with all that is. I can never be alone because I'm always connected to the Divine.

I am an Immortal Soul inhabiting an Ancient Tree. I remember seeing a red tail hawk sitting on a telephone pole one afternoon during a horrendous storm. Tears welled and my heart stuttered. "Oh my, that poor hawk!" I drove on for several miles before it dawned on me. Poor Hawk? I will admit I'm an animist but really! Did I truly think this hawk had a warm and cozy house with central heating and a hot toddy waiting for it once it found its afternoon snack?

Like the ancient trees and the red tail hawk, I've been buffeted by the vicissitudes of life. I've lived through snow and ice, rain and wind, drought, and floods. And like the trees and hawk I have survived them all. And through my survival, through being bent and bowed, I've become stronger. For a time last year, I forgot that strength, that core that survived disasters, challenges and the pain that attends them, but it was there when I chose to look.

I am an Immortal Soul inhabiting an Ancient Tree.

The words to this meditation still resonate with me on a visceral level. Even though in my late teens I thought of suicide, during the pandemic, I reached an even lower point.

What can be lower than contemplating suicide?

Questioning myself and not in a kind and compassionate way.

Questioning every major decision I'd made my entire life. And at the advanced age of 79 there were a myriad of them.

As I write this, I'm remembering my life one year ago. In that dark, dark time, I wasn't as alone in fact as it felt. One friend assisted me in getting appointments to be vaccinated and even drove me to the drive-through clinic for both shots. I had cataract surgery scheduled, another friend drove across town to pick me up, take me to the clinic which was close to her home and then drove me back to my house once surgery was over. I did have and do have friends and yet I felt disconnected.

Disconnected and despondent. Getting out of bed, getting dressed and feeding myself on some days was all I did. On good days I took a walk.

Reading? That took a level of concentration I didn't have. Even rereading favorites didn't help. I've no idea what I did for hours each day as weeks and then months passed by. I'd never experienced the level of despondency and despair over such a long period of time before.

What changed? As I've mentioned, I decided to attend Colette's 2021 event. My best friend came to stay at my house so we could share the experience. Even though my very best friend was with me, the emptiness, the disconnection on some level remained.

I'm an author and do workshops and training. I wrote a book *Staying Sane in a Crazy World* about how to stay sane in crazy times. It sat on a shelf along with my other books. Exercises during that virtual event reminded me I had resources, skills and ideas to move through, around and over obstacles but I wasn't using them.

For me, my answer came from tapping into my curiosity. These are the key questions I asked myself.

What did I want?

Which of my skills could I employ that would move me in that direction?

What was the underlying fear that kept me immobilized?

During one of the exercises, I saw myself at 100 living alone. No one with me. And it shook me to the core. I'd just been through a year of isolation and the image of that being my life when I came to the end was devastating...and yet? It stopped me in my tracks and led to some deep introspection, but it was not what had sent me down the slippery slope into the deep black well of despair.

There was another issue that impacted my sense of safety other than COVID: the reality that a fundamental layer in the foundation of my life was cracked and broken and might never be repaired. I was vaccinated, wore a mask and sanitized my house and car and still I lived in fear.

It wasn't COVID.

I got caught up in politics and fear.

Time to draw upon the experiences I've accumulated over the decades of my life. I called upon my old friend, *Curiosity*. And its partner *Memory*. Over the months of COVID I'd lost track of my Core Values. I'd written them down a decade or two ago. I looked and searched and looked some more but could find no trace.

My Core Values are at the heart of who I am and what I strive to live by.

Where were they?

Who knew the answer to that question? I certainly didn't.

Last fall, I sat down one afternoon with pen and a pad of paper and wrote them out again. When I look the list over, I have a sense of *coming home.* A sense that my world is in balance again. Living my life, making choices in congruence with my Core Values has always been and forever will be a good decision.

My Core Values

We are all connected to The Divine and thus are threads in The Fabric of The Universe which means we are all Sacred.

We each have our life path and have the right to traverse it without righteous interference from others.

Everything happens in "right time" and serves my highest good.

All experiences have a "gift" in them. It is my responsibility to find it.

We each have "Free Will" in how we perceive and respond to life events.

We are all doing the best we can given our past and present life experiences, our goals/dreams/wants.

The Universe/Spirit listens to my thoughts, words, prayers and it is up to me to be open to a different way for answers to come to me.

My life works better for me when I keep focused on Gratitude for what I have and call upon Wise Compassion and remembering we are all part of The Divine and thus Sacred.

There is enough of whatever I need.

I spent hours reflecting on my core values and contemplating the prospect of once again living my life in accordance with them by moving into radical trust, believing that by living with, being congruent with them would see me through to wherever my end is.

Sometimes we need to live in the darkness in order to appreciate the light.

And even in the darkness, remembering we are not alone shows us a pinprick of light so we know our way.

I am an Immortal Soul inhabiting an Ancient Tree. I am an Emissary for and a Spark of the Divine. Spirit has a plan for me. My connection to Spirit, to the Divine Matrix, to The Universe is now and forever more. I am not and never will be alone.

As this book is being published, Judith Ashley is celebrating being in sacred women's circles for thirty years. She knows first-hand how important spirituality is when dealing with life's challenges. However, the COVID pandemic isolated her from her own women's circle and her spiritual practice suffered. Taking a page from the women in her Sacred Women's Circle series, Judith found her way back to her spiritual practice, rewrote her Core Values and successfully found a path through the COVID pandemic.

Grieving During a Pandemic

by Holly E. Stern

There was plenty of grief to go around in the year 2020. COVID-19 was turning everyone's life upside down, mine included. But I had another reason to grieve: the death of my beloved husband, Don, to Alzheimer's. Not unexpected, but nonetheless devastating. Looking back, I find it hard to distinguish which emotions pertained to my bereavement and which to the global catastrophe.

Here in the United States, the mid-March shutdown hit about five weeks after my husband died. By that time, I had taken care of most of the required paperwork and was trying to keep my life moving forward as best I could. My schedule was packed with a dozen days of disparate music rehearsals and performances.

I am a professional violinist and also sing in my church choir, which is an enjoyable combination until they try to occupy the same time frame. It required traveling, both solo and orchestral violin playing, and choral singing. To add further challenge, one of the choir pieces was about someone who had recently died. I've never figured out how to cry and sing at the same time.

There was a question, lurking somewhere in the back of my mind, whether packing so much into such a short period was a good idea...especially with the diversity of the commitments and the out-of-town travel...especially with my raw grief. Performing usually feels to me a bit like a high wire act, and Don's death inserted a whole new magnitude of possibilities to fall, to fail.

But beginning on the evening of March 11th and over the next few days, everything was canceled. By the 16th, we were totally shut down.

Don's Celebration of Life, which I'd set for the end of April, got moved to September 20th, the 33rd anniversary of our meeting. Then that, too, went by the wayside. I was offered a Zoom memorial service, but I remained adamant about waiting until we could gather in person to give him a good send-off. People talk about "closure," but I was in no hurry to close this chapter of my life.

What the pandemic did give me was time. And quiet. Space to process my loss. Over the past decade, I'd promised myself that, after Don's death, I would write a book about our Alzheimer's experience. I dove in, putting on paper the thoughts and stories that had been rambling through my brain. The writing gave a fullness to our history and excavated memories of my healthy husband before the disease. By sharing them, I hoped I could help someone else dealing with a loved one's dementia.

I still needed to cope with the fact that life without people to bump up against was truly weird. They say you learn by going off course and then correcting. But what if there are no guardrails when you veer too far in one direction? People were my guardrails. And I had to find a way to navigate this thing called grief.

Fortunately, my friends were game for walking or bike riding. We masked up, physically distanced, and went out, rain or shine. Sometimes we would get Thai take-out and eat it in my backyard. That area became my living room, until it was too cold and damp to be enjoyable. Happily, other friends had covered patios, sometimes even heated and furnished with electric blankets.

For a brief while, during good weather, I gave "open window" concerts on my violin. I texted my neighbors that, at 5:15 PM, I would open my windows and give a short performance. It was my way of offering an uplifting counterbalance to the pandemic that was slowly eroding our lives. Friends (and sometimes passersby) would gather in my driveway, a few with a festive glass of wine in hand, to let the music work its wonders.

Unfortunately, it was too soon after Don's death for me to sustain the amount of energy performing requires. Grief regained the upper hand. At one point, it felt like I had crashed into a wall. A blank wall. I decided not to fight it. It may have been gardening season, but I had hit a fallow period.

As the pandemic shutdown continued, I freaked out when I realized suddenly that I had not touched another living being in over two months! Grieving is one thing; isolation is another. They do not make good companions.

It was obviously time to replace our cat, Misty, who had died nearly two years earlier. I was not alone in my search for a pet, however. Adoption proved trickier than normal, as the animal shelters were flooded with requests. It seemed I would never make it to the top of the adoption list.

A friend recommended I get an adult male cat, as they are often extremely affectionate, but none of the males offered at the time sounded like the right fit. Most were either too old or with medical problems (I was not in a rescuing frame of mind at that point). In desperation, I asked Don if he could help find me a good kitty. You never know what powers the deceased might possess, and I was open to all the help I could get. Sitting down again at my computer, I decided there were two "somewhat" possibilities, so I filled out questionnaires for both.

The following day, I got a call from the Humane Society. I had made it to the top of the list! The cat in question did not have a good PR photo. Someone had given him a lion cut, with fur on only his head, legs, and the end of his tail. He was a mystery kitty; little was known about his past. BUT, he was in good health, about a year old, and very affectionate. I signed up for a meet-and-greet the next day. As I drove him home from the shelter, I introduced him to Beethoven's Seventh Symphony on the radio and was pleased to discover my new housemate did not object to classical music. This was an excellent sign.

For those of you with inquiring minds, Theo the Cat's fur grew out, not all at once, but beginning at the nape of his neck and slowly inching its way toward his tail. Meanwhile, on the tail, the fur crept down from the end "poof," till the two camps met about an inch south of his body. In a shutdown, you have time to notice these things, and I'm happy to report that isolation is so much more manageable when you have a cat purring against you.

Then there were the Zoom meetings. God bless ingenuity. Suddenly the world was coming into our homes. This suited the part of me that hates wasted effort. Now I could take classes, listen to concerts, and join groups without having to commute. Learning about racial injustice and spiritual deepening was a fine use of a year when most of my music-making (aside from a virtual choir) was put on hold. In a way, I was growing myself out of my grief. And I could feel Don cheering me on.

After more than two years and many delays, we held a Celebration of Life for Don! It fell on May Day, which coincided with World Laughter Day, a perfect combination for my husband. The long hiatus proved a blessing. I was finally able to turn from grieving to embracing the celebration he deserved.

I wonder how I might have fared without the shutdown. That time was immeasurably rich for me. I now have many new friends, a more profound appreciation of the importance of connectedness, and a realization of what I need for a good mental outlook. Had life proceeded at its normal pace, I might have spent much more effort in just trying to keep up, nibbling away at my grief in between other activities.

I don't want in any way to minimize the heartbreak and devastation COVID-19 has wreaked on the world. This is not an attempt to glory in the shutdown. I was simply fortunate that the time and space it afforded me was exactly what I needed to deal with my own private grief.

Holly Stern is a native Oregonian who has made her career as a classical violinist, playing with the Portland Baroque Orchestra, Oregon Bach Festival, Portland Opera, and Oregon Ballet Theater. In addition, she taught at the University of Portland, the Community Music Center, and privately. Writing has been a lifelong passion of Holly's. "Grieving During a Pandemic" is an adaptation of a chapter from her book, Small Triumphs: Lessons in Alzheimer's and Love, *soon to be published. Holly also enjoys gardening, hiking, biking, and reading good books on the couch with Theo the Cat.*

NOT Summer Camp

by Mary Orr

Note from Paul—I received this May 16ᵗʰ email from my friend, Mary, just as we were finishing up editing our last story for this anthology. I did not know that Mary had been going through all of these issues with her husband, Michael. Having worked in the aging field for many years, I know how exhausting 24/7 caregiving can be—sleep deprivation, completing countless forms for assistance, touring facilities, etc.

I immediately responded to Mary's email and asked if there was anything I could do to help. But I realized there was something more to her email. She wrote with such raw emotion I felt it belonged in our anthology, but how? I couldn't ask someone who was as over-extended as she was to write a story. Then it became clear to me that email can be a modern-day form of storytelling.

I called Mary the next day and we talked on the phone for an hour and a half. At times it was comical as Mary was navigating the ride home from visiting Michael—getting off one bus, boarding another, walking home, making peppermint tea for her upset stomach, and heating up dinner. She is one resilient soul. I told Mary about this anthology project and how I would love to have her story added to our anthology. I also realized she had NO TIME to write her story. As a result, these two emails will stand on their own, with her gradual blessing. Her emails tell her story. I believe her writing demonstrates love and conviction during unimaginable circumstances.

April 21, 2022

Hello dear friends,

There are about 50 of you on this email (local, out-of-state, out-of-country); please forgive the group message. And, my usual chant: please forgive lack of correspondence.

You have different degrees of awareness of the last couple of years of Michael's decline and my 24/7 caregiving (and tortuous Medicaid application process), including hand-wringing blow-by-blow descriptions (sorry!). Your welcome visits, errand-running, home repair, and previous outings gave me respite before I had some regular in-home care (started in February). Thank you so much.

Even with the 30 hours/week care help I'm unable to care for Michael at home and my goal was always to move him to care. With support from a wise friend, I debated between adult family-style care homes with just 5 residents, and larger institutions, and chose the latter because they can care for him through all stages of Alzheimer's decline, and I won't need to move him. And they have dedicated night staff–a requirement for midnight wanderers. Most of both types of facilities are in the outer reaches of Portland, re-quiring about three hours (round trip) multi-bus travel.

I found Emerson House, located in urban Portland, much closer to me and to Michael's friends. At first, I rejected this three-story building. If there was another COVID lockdown we couldn't see each other, unlike at a single-story facility where I'd be able to peer through the ground-level window at a confused and stranded Michael. But Emerson assured me that they could set up video vis-its, and as feasible bring him down to the outdoor garden area, or to a first-floor window, where we could gaze, untouching. Not a kiss. Not a hand upon hand.

Every facility is like that in a lockdown. Reminds me of birds' demented attacks on windows, mistaking the reflection of vegetation in the window for an irresistible destination. Millions of birds die this way. And fragile Michael–his old self reaching, beseeching–is irresistible.

Getting him accepted there took several weeks. All of this, including changing his health care to a fabulous all-inclusive medical team specializing in elder care, and obtaining authority of his Social Security and the right to manage his money, has been a 24/7 job. And a roller coaster: on Monday I thought he wouldn't get into Emerson. On Tuesday he was accepted.

Then a COVID case forced a difficult decision: move in on schedule, gambling that it was better now than risking a potential longer delay or closure. The "great unmasked" are sending cases soaring, along with my blood pressure. I know many of you have been through all this in one way or another.

Michael will move on Monday, May 2. I'll move his things (furniture, art) the day before. It's not going to be an easy transition, and I'm really sad but it's the right thing to do. Michael is still Michael, with a sense of humor and love of visitors and outings, so later I'll talk with those of you in Portland about visiting him, especially in the first few months when it will be so helpful to him. I'll be visiting most days unless he's so angry that I need to lie low for a while.

Emerson has a temperature check device, tests staff and residents, and advises if there's a COVID case. COVID runs through our lives like that horrid song you can't get out of your head. Details to come, but if you're uncomfortable being indoors on the residents' floor (you must wear a mask), you can sit without a mask on the balcony, or the staff will bring Michael down to the conference room, or to the outdoor garden area once the furniture is set up. Don't let anyone you don't know into the elevator with you, or out of the locked building. Some residents can masquerade as visitors; that's what I would do if I were in there.

MICHAEL DOES NOT KNOW ABOUT THIS AND WILL NOT KNOW UNTIL HE ENTERS THE BUILDING.

My life will change too. I must say, I look forward to finishing a book, an article. Watching a program with a plot. Having an uninterrupted phone call. Getting enough sleep. Walking out the door without having to coordinate anything or anybody. Being able to help YOU. Or just doing nothing.

I'll miss my dear Michael, and it is heart-wrenching, but I'll be seeing him a lot and once he settles in it will be best for both of us. I've had a huge amount of support from experts, support groups, my amazing elder law attorney, and friends. Couldn't have done it without you.

Love to you all, and I'll be in touch. I hope your lives are chugging along. I won't be going on trips anytime soon, not with the maskless on public transportation. But at some point, I'll be on your doorstep, and I can hardly wait.

—Mary

**

May 16, 2022

Hello again friends and family,

Most of you heard about my plan to move Michael to Emerson House (memory care) on May 2. My distribution list wasn't complete so I filled in my recipient gaps haphazardly--so for some of you this message will come as news, but not a surprise. I'm so grateful for your caring support and heartfelt notes. I'm slowly responding to everyone--again haphazardly--but I'm thinking of you all with appreciation and recognition at how lucky we are to know you.

Dear friends whisked Michael away on May 1 to a day-long "party." Meanwhile, moving his things to his new room at Emerson went smoothly thanks to generous friends who gave up their

Sunday: hardworking movers, decorators, and labelers (every single item needed to be labeled with his name, like summer camp for the elderly).

Leaving Michael there on May 2 was NOT smooth (ask if you want the details). But thank you Mike from the poker group for bravely and compassionately joining me on that painful day.

Michael is starting to participate in Emerson's engaging activities such as "Art Therapy," "Horticulture," "Movin' and Groovin" and "Tea Time." On one visit we danced during "Sing-along," and he was so incredibly happy.

But I'm sure that Michael does NOT think it's summer camp. The transition has been difficult, as it would be for anyone moving from the comforts of home to an institution of strangers. It will get better once he adjusts, but during these first two weeks he's roamed the halls and common room some nights yelling and swearing and calling out for me, demanding I bring him home. Or forlornly dragging his blanket and pillow around, looking for a place to set up camp.

As is typical, they asked that I stay away for at least a week, but he was suffering so terribly and behaving so badly that after one week we (his health care team and Emerson staff) figured I couldn't make it any worse so I visited. Half of my visits have been quite lovely, and a couple of times the clouds have parted, and he's asked that I be honest and tell him what's going on and why he's there. I answer with a softened truth, and he accepts. But an hour later, or the next day, it's back to "THERE'S NO REASON I'M HERE AND IF YOU DON'T TAKE ME HOME, I'M GOING TO LEAVE." There's no "worst disease" but I nominate Alzheimer's anyway.

Oh, and to make matters worse, he's been diagnosed with Parkinson's too, so he has difficulty with balance though he uses a walker now. Let me know if you find one with power steering.

To relieve Michael's agitation and distress, he's on some pretty powerful drugs. His health care team is committed to using non-drug methods to guide behavior, and their goal is to use the drugs only on an "as needed basis" once he's more adjusted. It could take some time. It took him a year and a half to get over the loss of his driver's license and car (on a less powerful drug), and it was brutal.

By this point in our lives, just about everyone knows (or knew) someone with dementia (or young children!). The non-drug behavior techniques include redirecting, reassuring, etc., and you can read about those all over the web. It takes a LOT of energy and 100% kindness, so it's exhausting.

Special thanks to my high-school friend Claire, who has worked in a memory care facility and has spent hours helping me understand how to maneuver.

The caregiver crisis existed before COVID, but now it's beyond a crisis and I figure if Amazon and Starbucks workers can organize, so can the caregivers, who do a remarkable job (the union I belonged to had a few caregiver locals). But unions can only do so much in a neglected field: priorities, laws, and funding must be changed to build facilities, provide financial assistance for services, and pay a family wage for those caring for the vulnerable, the young, the elders, the disabled. I know, dream on. We all know the dream. But when you're on this draining journey navigating a frightening future; tangled and cruel bureaucracies; a bereft partner who's lost himself, his life, and his home; and the new world of memory care with its COVID isolation and video support groups–it's the medical care team, social workers, going-the-extra-mile government workers, and caregivers who shine and make it bearable.

Emerson employees--all of whom wear multiple hats–are compassionate, patient and skilled. They run a community. Michael is so lucky to have this new home, but the recent increase in COVID cases forces the staff to wear masks and face shields, so he must speculate whether they're bug exterminators or nuclear technicians. No wonder he asks, "What am I doing here?"

OK, this is long past appropriate reading length. I won't send missives every time Michael sneezes (unless it's COVID!) and please let me know if you'd rather not be on this list or prefer another way to communicate. LOL, there's always the "delete" key! I look forward to phone calls and visits, but I'm taking a shortcut now with this group update. Thanks for understanding.

All for now. I wish I had cheerier news, but we'll get there.

—Mary

Mary worked in a subarctic asbestos mine, at a women's shelter, and as a union activist.

She met her husband Michael at KBOO Community Radio in Portland, Oregon in 1977. They envisioned a retired life of road trips, working for social change, and backpacking until age 85. Instead, Mary is caring for Michael and rearranging her life.

Michael was a music recording engineer and oral historian. He has forgotten all his work, but it lives on digitally and on vinyl.

Mary wonders if people living with Alzheimer's informed the development of Buddhism, teaching detachment and living in the moment. And when Michael wanders the halls of the memory care center searching for Mary in the night, she wonders if, long ago, this is how haunting ghost stories emerged.

About the Editor

Paul Iarrobino is known for creating memorable experiences by weaving together personal narratives with grit and humor and coaching others to do the same. Paul added "author" to his storytelling wheelhouse, with the release of his first book, COVIDOLOGY: Sharing Life Lessons from Behind the Mask. *The vision for this anthology was sparked by a series of weekly virtual social support calls Paul facilitated throughout the pandemic. This anthology reflects the voices of many first-time storytellers navigating the pandemic and learning about themselves and others during an ever-changing landscape.*

Our Bold Voices

Paul encourages you to stay connected by visiting him at https://www.ourboldvoices.com. You can follow his work or sign up for occasional newsletter updates.

Windtree Press

Paul is one of several authors of this writing collective. For more books of the heart, go to Windtree Press at https://windtreepress.com.

Made in USA - Crawfordsville, IN
39110_9781957638294
01.31.2023 1539